The Confederate Book of Quotes & Narratives

By Richard Lee Montgomery

Wake Forest, NC

The Confederate Book of Quotes & Narratives

©2014 Richard Lee Montgomery

First Printing

The Scuppernong Press
PO Box 1724
Wake Forest, NC 27588
www.scuppernongpress.com

Cover and book design by Frank B. Powell, III

All rights reserved. Printed in the United States of America.

No part of this book may be reproduced or transmitted in any form or by any means, electronic or mechanical, including photocopying, recording, or by any information and storage and retrieval system, without written permission from the editor and/or publisher.

International Standard Book Number ISBN 978-0-9898399-5-2

Library of Congress Control Number: 2014939023

Table of Contents

Introduction 1

Politicians of the Confederacy 5

Soldiers of the Confederacy 35

Women of the Confederacy 95

Chaplains, Evangelist and Colporters of the Confederacy
.... 115

Bibliography 139

Index 155

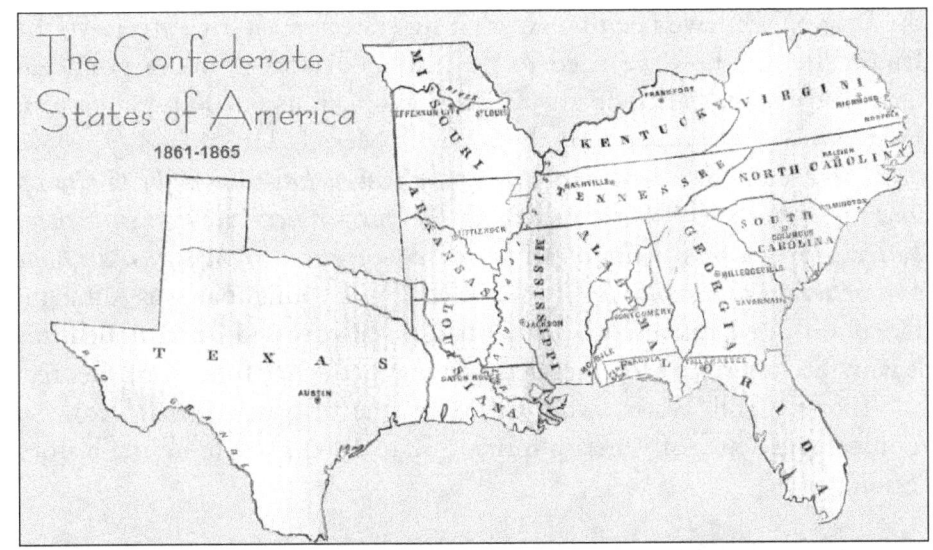

Introduction

"The first step in liquidating a people is to erase its memory. Destroy its books, its culture, its history. Then have somebody write new books, manufacture a new culture, invent a new history. Before long the nation will begin to forget what it is and what it was." [1]
Milan Kundera

The hope for this book is to show the narrative of the day when the South was invaded by those who desired to inflict their ideals, morals and attitudes, just because "these Southerners" needed to be brought back under the Northerner's way of life, their philosophy of life and their interpretation of the law. But above all, it was because the Northerners way of life was jolted economically when the Southern states seceded from

---

[1] Andrea O'Reilly Herrera, *Remembering Cuba: Legacy of a Diaspora* (University of Texas Press, 2001), 20.

the Union. We have been taught that no state has the right to leave the Union, but oh how we need to be reminded what a young politician once said in his speech to the United States House of Representatives, January 12, 1848, concerning the war with Mexico. He said, *"Any people, anywhere, being inclined and having the power, have the right to rise up and shake off the existing government, and form a new one that suits them better. This is a most valuable, a most sacred right, a right which we hope and believe is to liberate the world."* [2] Well, this young man was Abraham Lincoln. But we can also go further back in history and be reminded this is why the American Colonies declared independence from King George.

Thomas Hill Watts, who served as the attorney general for the Confederate States of America from 1862 to 1863 gives us a brief history lesson:

> *"In the days of 1776, our forefathers declared that to secure life, liberty and the pursuit of happiness, 'Governments are instituted among men, deriving their powers from the consent of the governed; and that whenever any form of government becomes destructive of these ends, it is the right of the people to altar or abolish it, and to institute new government, laying its foundations on such principles, and organizing its powers in such form as to them shall seem most likely to affect their safety and happiness.*[3]

So, when the Union Army invaded the South, this did not set well with the people in the Southron. In fact, they were willing to fight for this "sacred" right to leave the Union. Attorney General Watts goes on:

> *"Because of the exercise of this right—a right lying at the foundation of all free government, and the corner stone of every republican system of government, the Northern States, now calling themselves the United States, made war on the Confederate States. The authorities of these Northern States by their declarations and their conduct thus deny the right of free government—deny that all governments derive their powers from the consent of the governed—deny the doctrines of the Declaration of*

---

[2] Roy P. Basler, *The Collected Works of Abraham Lincoln, Volume 1* (Rutgers University Press, New Brunswich, New Jersey, 1953), 431-42.

[3] *Inaugural Address of Gov. Thomas H. Watts Before the Alabama Legislature, December 1, 1863* (Montgomery: Montgomery Advertiser Book and Job Offices, 1863), 3.

Independence, and the principles of the fathers of the Republic, and assert and attempt to exercise the doctrines of force. They deny to the people of Alabama the right of self government, and declare the monstrous pharisaic dogma, that they have the right to coerce us to be subservient to their will! that they are our superiors our masters! and we, their inferiors! their slaves!" [4]

Point is, this mind set represented many Southerners in their homes, towns and states. This was the primary reason for secession. The desired hope for this book is that maybe it will help someone become familiar with the people of the South or for many, who are students of "all things Southern" will become more familiar with the people of the South.

There are many today who identify that our American history is not being presented the way it use to be. Revisionists are in abundance. From the early days of the "American Revolution" to the "War Between the States" and probably won't be long before "World War II" will come under the monstrous tool of political correction. Bottom line it is the right thing to be reminded of this narrative of the Southern people who stood for the right of state sovereignty. Hopefully, as you read these quotes and narratives, of which most come from primary sources, that it will bring us closer to the facts of history and erase the opinions, of the new order of modern historians, where facts are deemed as secondary. History can easily become a lie when interpreted by the opinions of men and then, what do you get? Certainly you get no facts. George Santayana hit the bulls eye when he said, "Those who cannot remember the past are condemned to repeat it.[5]

Listen to the attitudes expressed as you read. Count the times you sense a voice of strong conviction on moral issues, political advice and cultural lifestyle. If your roots are from the South, enjoy your heritage. But above all, let us not forget our Southern history and heritage.

---

[4] Ibid., 7.
[5] George Santayana, *The Life of Reason and the Phases of Human Progress* (New York: Charles Scribner's Sons, 2012) 284.

Politicians of the Confederacy

Jefferson Davis
Alexander Hamilton Stephens
Robert Augustus Toombs
Robert Mercer Taliaferro Hunter
Judah Philip Benjamin
Christopher Gustavus Memminger
John Henninger Reagan
Leroy Pope Walker
Stephen Russell Mallory
Thomas Hill Watts
George Davis
Robert Barnwell Rhett
Albert Gallatin Brown
Williamson Simpson Oldham
Gustavus A. Henry
William L. Yancey

"Nothing fills me with deeper sadness than to see a Southern man apologizing for the defense we made of our inheritance." [6]
Jefferson Davis

President Jefferson Finis Davis

"All we ask is to be let alone."[7]

"I love the Union and the Constitution, but I would rather leave the Union with the Constitution than remain in the Union without it." [8]

"We feel that our cause is just and holy; we protest solemnly in the face of mankind that we desire peace at any sacrifice save that of honor and independence; we seek no conquest, no aggrandizement, no concession of any kind from the States with which we were lately confederated; all we ask is to be let alone; that those who never held power over us shall not now attempt our subjugation by arms. This we will, this we must, resist to the direst extremity." [9]

US Senator, Jefferson Davis say on December 10, 1860: "I would have this Union severed into thirty three fragments sooner than have that great evil befall constitutional liberty and representative government. Our Government is an agency of delegated and strictly limited powers. Its founders did not look to its preservation by force; but the chain they wove to bind these States together was one of love and mutual good offices. They had broken the fetters

---

[6] Wilmer L. Jones, *Generals in Blue and Gray, Volume 2* (Stackpole Books, 2005), 34.

[7] Edward A. Pollard, *Life of Jefferson Davis, Secret History of the Southern Confederacy, Gathered Behind the Scenes in Richmond* (Atlanta: National Publishing Company, 1869), 137.

[8] John Thomas Nall, *God Save the South: And a Treasure Chest of Forbidden Information* (AuthorHouse, 2013), 478.

[9] Edward A. Pollard, *Life of Jefferson Davis, Secret History of the Southern Confederacy, Gathered Behind the Scenes in Richmond* (Atlanta: National Publishing Company, 1869), 137.

of despotic power; they had separated themselves from the mother-country upon the question of community independence...." [10]

"And yet you see we are driven to take up arms for the defense of our rights and liberties." [11]

"General Lee has asked for it. Congress has passed it. How then can I veto it?" [12]

"I must say that there never was ... a body of men less fitted for the task which they had undertaken than the first Congress.... Jealousy, selfish ambition and consequent discord prevailed from the commencement, and in a month after I took my seat in it, I would have resigned but for the dissuasion of my wife, who was devoted to the cause, and said that my resignation would be misunderstood and regarded as disaffection." [13]

"the danger is not that by these acquisitions we shall sow the seeds of disunion but ... rather that, by an inordinate acquisition, we shall sow the seeds of centralization." [14]

"Let us then unite our hands and our hearts, lock our shields together, and we may well believe that before another summer solstice falls upon us, it will be the enemy who will be asking us for conferences and occasions in which to make known our demands." [15]

"If instead of being a dissolution of a league, it were indeed a rebellion in which we are engaged, we might find ample vindication for the course we have adopted in the scenes which are now being enacted in the United States. Our people now look with contemptuous astonishment on those with whom

---

[10] Jefferson Davis, *The Rise and Fall of the Confederate Government, Volume 1* (New York: A. Appleton & Company, 1881), 63.

[11] Hudson Strode, *Jefferson Davis: Confederate President* (New York: Harcourt, Brace and Company, 1950), 74.

[12] Ibid., 388.

[13] Ibid., 205.

[14] Elisabeth Cutting, *Jefferson Davis: Political Soldier* (New York: Dodd, Mead & Company, 1930), 102.

[15] Ibid., 236.

they had been so recently associated. They shrink with aversion from the bare idea of renewing such a connection. When they see a President making war without the assent of Congress ; when they behold judges threatened because they maintain the writ of habeas corpus so sacred to freedom; when they see justice and law trampled under the armed heel of military authority, and upright men and innocent women dragged to distant dungeons upon the mere edict of a despot; when they find all this tolerated and applauded by a people who had been in the full enjoyment of freedom but a few months ago—they believe that there must be some radical incompatibility between such a people and themselves. "With such a people we may be content to live at peace, but the separation is final, and for the independence we have asserted we will accept no alternative." [16]

"I am sorry to learn it. M., Lincoln was a much better man than his successor will be, and it will go harder with our people. It is bad news for us." [17]

"My physical condition rendered it obvious that there could be no idea that fetters were needful to the security of my imprisonment. It was clear, therefore, that the object was to offer an indignity both to myself and the cause I represented—not the less sacred to me because covered with the pall of a military disaster. It was for this reason I resisted as a duty to my faith, to my countrymen, and to myself. It was for this reason I courted death from the muskets of the guard. The officer of the day prevented that result, and, indeed, bowing-to Captain Titlow, behaved like a man of good feelings. Patriots in all ages, to whose memories shrines are now built, have suffered as bad or worse indignities." [18]

"The women of the South had sent forth their sons, directing them to return with wounds disabling them for further service, or never to return at all. All they had flung into the contest—beauty, grace, passion, ornament; the exquisite frivolities so dear to the sex were cast aside; their songs, if they had any heart to sing, were patriotic; their trinkets were flung into the public

---

[16] William E. Dodd, *Jefferson Davis* (Philadelphia: George W. Jacobs & Company, 1907), 257-258.
[17] Varina Davis, *Jefferson Davis: Ex-President of the Confederate States of America, Volume 2* (New York: Belford Company, Publishers, 1890), 629.
[18] Ibid., 663.

crucible; the carpets from their floors were portioned out as blankets to the suffering soldiers of their cause; women bred to every refinement of luxury, wore home-spuns made by their own hands; when materials for an armyballoon were wanted, the richest silk dresses were sent in, and there was only competition to secure their acceptance. As nurses of the sick, as encouragers and providers for the combatants, as angels of charity and mercy, adopting as their own all children made orphans in defence of their homes, as patient and beautiful household deities, accepting every sacrifice with unconcern, and lightening the burdens of war by every art, blandishment, and labor proper to their sphere, the dear women of his people deserved to take rank with the highest heroines of the grandest days of the greatest countries." [19]

From prison to Richmond—"I feel like an unhappy ghost visiting this much beloved city." [20]

"We have witnessed the organization of a party seeking the possession of the Government, not for the common good, not for their own particular benefit, but as the means of executing a hostile purpose against a portion of the States." [21]

"Believing the States to be each sovereign, and their union voluntary, I had learned from the Fathers of the Constitution that a State could change its form of government, abolishing all which had previously existed; and my only crime has been obedience to this conscientious conviction. Was not this the universal doctrine of the dominant Democratic party in the North previous to secession? Did not many of the opponents of that party, in the same section, share and avow that faith? They preached and professed to believe. We believed, and preached, and practised." [22]

---

[19] Ibid., 683.
[20] Ibid., 794.
[21] Frank H. Alfriend, *The Life of Jefferson Davis* (Cincinnati: National Publishing House, 1868), 120.
[22] Markinfield Addey, *Life and Imprisonment of Jefferson Davis, Together With the Life and Military Career of Stonewall Jackson* (New York: M. Doolady, Publisher, 1866), 83.

Vice President Alexander Hamilton Stephens

"If centralism is ultimately to prevail; if our entire system of free Institutions as established by our common ancestors is to be subverted, and an Empire is to be established in their stead; if that is to be the last scene of the great tragic drama now being enacted: then, be assured, that we of the South will be acquitted, not only in our own consciences, but in the judgment of mankind, of all responsibility for so terrible a catastrophe, and from all guilt of so great a crime against humanity."[23]

"The real cause of the war, as set forth in the issue presented by me, condensed in a few words, was the denial of the fact that ours was a Federal Government; that the violation of this fundamental principle of our complicated organization, on the part of those controlling the General Government at the time, by assuming that the United States constituted a nation of individuals, with a consolidated sovereignty in the central Government, to which the ultimate as well as primary allegiance of the citizens of the several States was due, and that any attempt by the several States, or any of them, to resume the sovereign powers which had been previously delegated, in trust only, by them to the federal agency, was rebellion on their part."[24]

"Question by the Reconstruction Committee: In 1861, when the Ordinance of Secession was adopted in your State, to what extent was it supported by the people?

Answer: After the proclamation of President Lincoln calling out seventy-five thousand militia, under the circumstances it was issued, and blockading the Southern ports, and the suspension of the writ of habeas corpus, the Southern Cause, as it was termed, received the almost unanimous support of the people of Georgia. Before that they were very much divided on the question of the policy of secession. But afterwards they supported the cause within the range of my knowledge, with very few exceptions (there were some few exceptions,

---

[23] Thomas E. Woods, Jr., *33 Questions About American History You're Not Supposed to Ask* (Random House LLC, 2007), 80.
[24] *A Review of the First Volume of Alexander H. Stephens's War Between the States By Constitutionalist* (Philadelphia: J. P. Lippincott & Company, 1872), 16.

not exceeding half a dozen, I think). The impression then prevailing was, that public liberty was endangered, and they supported the cause because of their zeal for constitutional rights." [25]

"Gentlemen and fellow-citizens, for though we met as strangers from different and independent States, we are once more citizens of a common country. [Applause.] Allow me briefly and sincerely to return you my unfeigned thanks for this compliment. The state of my health, my voice and the night air, apart from all other considerations, will prevent me from doing more. This is not the time or the-place to discuss those great questions which are now pressing upon our public counsels. We are in a transition condition in the process of a new formation. Sufficient to say, that this day a new republic has been born the Confederate States of America has been ushered into existence, to take its place amongst the nations of the earth [cheers] under a temporary or provisional government, it is true ; but soon to be followed by one of a permanent character, which, while it surrenders none of our ancient rights and liberties, will secure more perfectly, we trust, the peace, security, and domestic tranquility that should be the objects of all governments. [Applause.]" [26]

"It is as simple as the utterance of a word and that is the recognition of the sovereignty of the States. With this on the part of the northern government, the troubled waters would instantly subside. But I see no prospect for this. Indeed, had not that government violated this' fundamental principle of American constitutional liberty, there would have been no war. The southern States would have seceded. And if they had found that it was to their interest to remain to themselves, would have done so, and ought to have done so and if they had found that it was to their interest to be in union with their former confederates on the basis of the old compact, the reunion would have taken place voluntarily and peaceably, as it was at first effected." [27]

"My judgment, as is well-known, is against the policy of immediate secession

---

[25] Richard Malcolm Johnston and William Hand Browne, *Life of Alexander H. Stephens* (Philadelphia: J. P. Lippincott & Company, 1878), 595.
[26] Henry Cleveland, *Alexander H. Stephens in Public and Private With Letters and Speeches, Before, During, and Since the War* (National Publishing Company, 1886), 157.
[27] Ibid., 178.

for any existing causes. It cannot receive the sanction of my vote; but if the judgment of the majority of this convention, embodying as it does the Sovereignty of Georgia be against mine; if a majority of the delegates in this convention shall, by their votes, dissolve the compact of union which has connected her so long with her Confederate States, and to which I have been so ardently attached, and which I have made such efforts to continue and to perpetuate upon the principles on which it was founded, I shall bow in submission to that decision." [28]

"In the conflict thus far, success has been on our side, complete throughout the length and breadth of the Confederate States. It is upon this, as I have stated, our social fabric is firmly planted; and I cannot permit myself to doubt the ultimate success of a full recognition of this principle throughout the civilized and enlightened world." [29]

"The great objects of humanity are best attained when there is conformity to his laws and decrees, in the formation of governments as well as in all things else. Our confederacy is founded upon principles in strict conformity with these laws. This stone which was rejected by the first builders ' is become the chief of the corner — the real corner-stone — in our new edifice." [30]

"I have always regarded him as the ablest man in our army; indeed, the first military man on the continent. The last time Mr. Davis consulted me on any question was about who should be sent to command at Charleston. I urged him to send Lee. Lee was sent. This was in November, 1861.... I was wonderfully taken with Lee in our first interview. I saw him put to the test that tries character. He came out of the crucible, pure and refined gold." [31]

"The consternation that has come upon the people is the result of a sectional election of a President of the United States, one whose opinions and avowed principles are in antagonism to our interests and rights...." [32]

---

[28] Frank H. Norton, *The life of Alexander H. Stephens* (New York: John B. Alden, Publisher, 1886), 45-46.

[29] Ibid., 52.

[30] Ibid., 53.

[31] Myrta Lockett Avary, *Recollections of Alexander H. Stephens* (New York: Doubleday, Page & Company, 1910), 80-81.

[32] Rudolph Von Abele, *Alexander H Stephens: A Biography* (New York: Alfred A. Knopf, 1946), 4-5.

Secretary of State (1861)
Robert Augustus Toombs

"We have not sought this conflict; we have sought too long to avoid it; our forbearance has been construed into weakness, our magnanimity into fear, until the vindication of our manhood, as well as the defence of our rights, is required at our hands."[33]

"There are courageous and honest men enough in both sections to fight. There is no question of courage involved. The people of both sections of this Union have illustrated their courage on too many battlefields to be questioned. They have shown their fighting qualities shoulder to shoulder whenever their country has called upon them; but that they may never come in contact with each other in fratricidal war, should be the ardent wish of every true man and honest patriot."[34]

"If there is any faith in man, we may rely on the assurances we have as to the status. Time is essential to the principal issue of this mission. In the present posture of affairs, precipitation is war."[35]

"Mr. President, at this time, it is suicide, murder, and will lose us every friend at the North. You will wantonly strike a hornet's nest which extends from mountains to ocean, and legions, now quiet, will swarm out and sting us to death. It is unnecessary; it puts us in the wrong; it is fatal."[36]

"One of my regiments, the 17th Georgia, had a skirmish day before yesterday. They acted splendidly, charging the Yankees, and driving them from the rifle-pits, killing, wounding, and taking prisoners over one hundred of the enemy. I lost but two killed and a few wounded."[37]

---

[33] *Speech of Hon. Robert Toombs: On the Crisis. Delivered Before the Georgia Legislature, December 7, 1860* (Lemuel Towers, 1860), 3.

[34] Pleasant A. Stovall, *Robert Toombs: Statesmen, Speaker, Soldier, Sage* (New York: Cassell Publishing Company, 1892), v.

[35] Ibid., 223.

[36] Ibid., 226.

[37] Ibid., 244.

"I think it requires as great qualifications to govern this country as it does to be a brigadier general."[38]

"Go it, boys! I am with you again. Jeff Davis can make a general, but it takes God Almighty, to make a soldier!"[39]

"You will not regard confederate obligations; you will not regard constitutional obligations; you will not regard your oaths. What, then, am I to do? Am I a freeman? Is my state, a free state, to lie down and submit because political fossils raise the cry of the glorious Union? Too long already have we listened to this delusive song? We are freemen. We have rights; I have stated them. We have wrongs; I have recounted them. I have demonstrated that the party now coming into power has declared us outlaws and is determined to exclude four thousand million of our property from the common territories; that it has declared us under the ban of the empire and out of the protection of the laws of the United States everywhere. They have refused to protect us from invasion and insurrection by the federal power, and the Constitution denies to us in the Union the right either to raise fleets or armies for our own defense. All these charges I have proven by the record; and I put them before the civilized world, and demand the judgment of today, of tomorrow, of distant ages, and of Heaven itself, upon the justice of these causes. I am content, whatever it be, to peril all in so noble, so holy a cause. We have appealed, time and time again, for these constitutional rights. You have refused them. We appeal again. Restore us these rights as we had them, as your court adjudges them to be, just as all our people have said they are; redress these flagrant wrongs, seen of all men, and it will restore fraternity, and peace, and unity, to all of us. Refuse them and what then? We shall then ask you, 'Let us depart in peace.' Refuse that, and you present us war. We accept it, and inscribing upon our banners the glorious words 'liberty and equality,' we will trust to the blood of the brave and the God of battles for security and tranquillity."[40]

"Nobody is strong enough to keep me out of Fort Warren except Johnson. All the Supreme Court could not do it if they wanted to do so. 'The life

---

[38] Ibid., 247.
[39] Ibid., 261-262.
[40] Ulrich Bonnell Philips, *The Life of Robert Toombs* (New York: The MacMillan Company, 1913), 218-219.

of the nation' would be adjudged by the commander-in-chief to require incarceration; and if anything more was deemed needful to the 'life of the nation,' a military court could hang me much more rightfully than it could the poor woman (Mrs. Surratt I believe) who was hung in Washington; for I did try to take 'the life of the nation,' and sorely regret the failure to do it."[41]

"*The basis, the corner-stone of this government, was the perfect equality of the free, sovereign, and independent States which made.*"[42]

Secretary of State (1861-1862)
Robert Mercer Taliaferro Hunter

"*I, for one, would be willing to regulate the right of secession, which I hold to be a right not given in the Constitution, but resulting from the nature of the compact.*"[43]

"*I do not say that this right of secession is laid down in the Constitution. It results from the nature of the compact. When two nations enter into a treaty of mutual obligations, and one fails to fulfill its part, the other may cancel it; not from any stipulation in the treaty, but from the nature of the compact. It is the very remedy for the very wrong; and, indeed, it is the only remedy for the wrong.*"[44]

"*Secession does not necessarily destroy the Union, or rather the hopes of reunion; it may turn out to be the necessary path to reconstruction.*"[45]

---

[41] Ibid., 255.

[42] *Speech of Hon. Robert Toombs: On the Crisis. Delivered Before the Georgia Legislature, December 7, 1860* (Lemuel Towers, 1860), 3.

[43] *Speech of Hon. R. M. T. Hunter, of Virginia, On the Resolution Proposing to Retrocede the Forts, Dock-Yards, to the States Applying For the Same* (January 11, 1861), 8.

[44] Ibid., 10.

[45] Ibid., 14.

Secretary of State (1861-1865)
Judah Philip Benjamin

"I speak, gentlemen in the belief that our independence is not to be maintained without the shedding of our blood. I know that the conviction is not shared by others. Heaven grant that I may prove mistaken. Yet fearful as is the ordeal, and much as war is to be deplored, it is not the unmixed evil which many consider it to be."[46]

"It is a revolution; a revolution of the most intense character; in which belief in the justice, prudence, and wisdom of secession is blended with the keenest sense of wrong and outrage, and it can no more be checked by human effort for the time than a prairie fire by a gardener's watering pot."[47]

"You do not propose to enter into our States, you say, and what do we complain of? You do not pretend to enter into our States to kill or destroy our institutions by force. Oh, no... You propose simply to close us in an embrace that will suffocate us... The day for adjustment has passed... We desire, we beseech you, let this parting be in peace... you can never subjugate us; you can never convert the free sons of the soil into vassals, paying tribute to your power; and you never, never can degrade them to the level of an inferior and servile race. Never! Never!"[48]

Secretary of the Treasury (1861-1864)
Christopher Gustavus Memminger

"Our Country — Our Whole Country: Not circumscribed within the narrow confines of a single State, but co-extensive with the broad expanse of our glorious confederacy."[49]

---

[46] Pierce Butler, *Judah P. Benjamin* (Philadelphia: George W. Jacobs & Company Publishers, 1906), 226.

[47] Thomas W. Cutrer, T. Michael Parrish, *Brothers in Gray: The Civil War Letters of the Pierson Family* (LSU Press, 2004), 4.

[48] Speech of Hon. J. P. Benjamin, of Louisiana, on the right of secession delivered in the Senate of the United States, Dec. 31, 1860, pages 15-16.

[49] Henry D. Capers, *The life and Times of Christopher Gustavus Memminger* (Richmond: Everett Waddey Company, Publishers.1893), 70.

"Whenever any form of government becomes destructive of the ends for which it was established, it is the right of the people to alter or abolish it and to institute a new government."[50]

"I cannot hold to the monstrous doctrine that any single State has the right under the Constitution to put her veto upon a law of the general government, passed under all the prescribed forms, and yet remain a member of the Federal Union ; that one of a confederacy of twenty-four States can by her sole voice check the action of the government, and stay its arm in the vital operation of collecting its revenues. This doctrine seems to me to lead to consequences which threaten anarchy and misrule; it puts the State in direct opposition to those constituted authorities which are sworn to enforce the laws, and sets at defiance the very powers which were appointed to settle differences. To such a doctrine it is impossible for me to assent; nay, I feel bound utterly to reprobate a scheme which, unless arrested by the intelligence and patriotism of the people of this State, will bring ruin upon our happy institutions; for I see in it the rising tempest which threatens to overthrow the altar consecrated to Liberty and Union by the immortal 'Washington himself.'"[51]

"Let all the anti-tariff States, or at least the Atlantic portion of them south of the Potomac, make common cause ; as they have a common interest, they should be actuated by the same political impulse and feeling. Let, therefore, Virginia, North and South Carolina, Georgia, Mississippi, Alabama, and as many of the adjacent States as choose to join us, assemble in convention, if you please, and, acting in concert, present to the federal government the alternative of receding from its unjust and oppressive legislation or submission to our separation from the confederacy. I am fully aware of the hazard of such a proceeding. Should Congress adhere to its iniquitous policy, and we are driven to the necessity of pursuing the last and worse branch of the alternative, it is easy to imagine many dangers, difficulties, and expenses we should have to encounter."[52]

---

[50] Ibid., 290.
[51] Ibid., 76-77.
[52] Ibid., 82.

"If, as I solemnly believe, we can no longer live in peace and harmony in the Union—notwithstanding the associations of the past and the remembrance of our common triumphs (being treated as enemies and aliens, rather than brethren of the same family, and heirs of the same inheritance, by the North), we can form a confederacy with ability to protect itself against any enemy, and command the respect and admiration of the world."[53]

Secretary of the Treasury (1865), Postmaster General (1861-1865) John Henninger Reagan

"But I can tell you what your folly and injustice will compel us to do. It will compel us to be free from your domination, and more self-reliant than we have been."[54]

"I would rather have been able to say that I had been a worthy member of Hood's Texas Brigade than to have enjoyed all the honors which have been conferred upon me. I doubt if there has ever been a brigade, or other military organization in the history of the world, that equaled it in the heroic valor and self-sacrificing conduct of its members, and in the brilliancy of its services."[55]

"I stand here to-day to say that if there be a southern State, or a southern man even, who would demand, as a condition for remaining in this Union, anything beyond the clearly specified guarantees of the Constitution of the United States as they are, I do not know of it. I can speak for my own State (Texas). I think I have had intimate association enough with her people to declare that they have never dreamed of asking more than their constitutional rights. They are, however, unalterably determined never to submit to less than their constitutional rights; never, never, sir! You can rely upon that, Mr. Chairman."[56]

---

[53] Ibid., 240.
[54] John H. Reagan, *State of the Union. Speech of the Hon. John H. Reagan, of Texas* (Washington, D. C.: W. H. Moore, Printer, 1861), 8.
[55] J. B. Polley, *Hoods Texas Brigade: It's Marches, It's Battles, It's Achievements* (New York: The Neale Publishing Company, 1910), 287.
[56] John H. Reagan, *State of the Union. Speech of the Hon. John H. Reagan, of Texas* (Washington, D. C.: W. H. Moore, Printer, 1861), 9.

"You are not content with the vast millions of tribute we pay you annually under the operation of our revenue law, our navigation laws, your fishing bounties, and by making your people our manufacturers, our merchants, our shippers. You are not satisfied with the vast tribute we pay you to build up your great cities, your railroads, your canals. You are not satisfied with the millions of tribute we have been paying on account of the balance of exchange which you hold against us. You are not satisfied that we of the South are almost reduced to the condition of overseers for Northern capitalists. You are not satisfied with all this; but you must wage a relentless crusade against our rights and institutions."[57]

"The irrepressible conflict propounded by abolitionism has produced now its legitimate fruits — disunion."[58]

"When the Southern members appealed to those from the North to aid them in some measure of peace which would preserve the Constitution and preserve the rights of the States and of the people of the South, such appeals were answered by the statement, 'We are in the majority and you will have to submit.' The Southern members and the Southern people did not want secession—they only sought the protection which was due them under the provisions of the Constitution. The Southern people had always shown their devotion to the Union, even while the New Englanders were threatening secession and disunion."[59]

"In the prior history of the country repeated instances are found of the assertion of the right of secession and of a purpose entertained at various times to put it into execution. Notably is this true of Massachusetts—indeed, of all New England. In 1786, when the States were bound by the Articles of Confederation, we are told that the situation was 'dangerous in the extreme.' The agitation in Massachusetts was great and it was declared that if Jay's negotiations, closing the Mississippi for twenty years, could not be adopted, it was high time for the New England States to secede from the Union and form a confederation for themselves. Plumer traces secession movements in 1792 and 1794, and says, 'All dissatisfied with the measures of the

---

[57] John H. Reagan, *Memoirs, With Special Reference to Secession and the Civil War* (New York: The Neale Publishing Company, 1906), 260-261.
[58] Ibid., 261.
[59] Ibid., 90-91.

government looked to a separation of the States as a remedy for oppressive grievances.' In 1794 Fisher Ames said: 'The spirit of insurrection has tainted a vast amount of country besides Pennsylvania.' In 1796 Governor Wolcott of Connecticut said: 'I sincerely declare that I wish the Northern States would separate from the Southern States the moment that event [the election of Jefferson] shall take place.' Horatio Seymour, on October 8, 1880, in a public address in New York City, thus spoke: 'The first threat of disunion was uttered upon the floor of Congress by Josiah Quincy, one of the most able and distinguished sons of Massachusetts. At an early day Mr. Hamilton, with all his distrust of the Constitution, sent word to the citizens of Boston to stop their threats of disunion and let the government stand as long as it would. When our country was engaged with the superior power, population, and resources of Great Britain, when its armies were upon our soil, when the walls of its capitol were blackened and marred by the fires kindled by our foes, and our Union was threatened with disaster, the leading officials of New England threatened resistance to the military measures of the Administration. This was the language held by a convention of delegates appointed by the legislatures of three New England States and by delegates from counties in Vermont: In cases of deliberate, dangerous, and palpable infraction of the Constitution, affecting the sovereignty of a State, and liberties of the people, it is not only right but the duty of such State to interpose for their protection in the manner best calculated to secure that end. This covers the whole doctrine of nullification. 'I may add, it covers the whole doctrine of secession, for it recognized the right of the State to determine when infractions of the Constitution have occurred, and to apply their own remedies.' The men who uttered these threats, which gave 'aid and comfort' to the enemies of this country while they were burning its capitol, were held in high esteem. To this day the names of George Cabot, Nathan Dove, Roger M. Sherman, and their associates are honored in New England. The acquisition of Louisiana, in 1803, created much dissatisfaction throughout New England, for the reason, as expressed by George Cabot, Senator from Massachusetts, and the grandfather of Senator Henry Cabot Lodge (in whose Life of George 'Cabot the statement is made): 'That the influence of our (northeastern) part of the Union must be diminished by the acquisition of more weight at the other extremity.' At the time secession, or the separation of the States, was freely discussed with no suggestion of any idea among its advocates that it was treasonable or revolutionary.'"[60]

---

[60] Ibid., 98-99.

"I need offer no apology for making this long quotation, which fully sustains my briefer reference to important facts of history; and shows very conclusively that the people of that part of the Union now entertain very different views as to the right of a State to secede, from those they formerly advocated. Their arguments of late years, on this question, would convict their fathers of threatened revolution and treason, which would seem to be rather unfilial; and creates a suspicion of hypocrisy, and can hardly be classed as political honesty. It is a note worthy fact that while the representatives of the other States disapproved and condemned these threats of secession, they never denied the right of a State to secede when there was no other remedy against wrongs and oppressions."[61]

"The purpose of my letter was to aid in securing the release of President Davis from prison. I urged that the welfare of the whole country would be subserved by setting him free without a trial; for the South it would be a signal that harsh and vindictive measures were to be relaxed; and for the North it would indicate that they were willing to let the decision of the right of secession rest where it was and not try to secure a judicial verdict."[62]

Secretary of War (1861)
Leroy Pope Walker

"... there was only one man there who had any sense and this man was Benjamin. Mr. Benjamin proposed that the Government purchase as much cotton as it could hold, at least 100,000 bales, and ship it at once to England. With the proceeds of a part of it he advised the immediate purchase of at least 150,000 stands of arms, and guns and munitions in corresponding amount. The residue of the cotton to be held as a basis for credit. For, said Benjamin, we are entering on a contest that may be long and costly. All the rest of us fairly ridiculed the idea of a serious war. Well, you know what happened."[63]

---

[61] Ibid., 101.
[62] Ibid., 231.
[63] Burton J. Hendrick, *Statesmen Of The Lost Cause Jefferson Davis And His Cabinet* (New York: The Literary Guild of America, Inc., 1939), 203.

Secretary of the Navy (1861-1865)
Stephen Russell Mallory

"It is not for me to indicate the path she [the South] may, in her wisdom, pursue; but, sir, my whole heart is with her, and she will find me treading it with undivided affections."[64]

"I regard the possession of an iron-armored ship as a matter of the first necessity. Such a vessel at this time could traverse the entire coast of the United States, prevent all blockades, and encounter, with a fair prospect of success, their entire navy."[65]

"It was recognized by Secretary Mallory in his report of November 20, 1861, that 'iron-clad steamships capable of resisting the crushing weight of projectiles from heavy ordnance must at- an early day constitute the principal part of the fighting vessels of all naval powers ... '"[66]

"The Virginia is a novelty in naval construction, is untried, and her powers unknown; and hence the department will not give specific orders as to her attack upon the enemy. Her powers as a ram are regarded as very formidable, and it is hoped you will be able to test them. Like the bayonet charge of infantry, this mode of attack, while the most destructive, will commend itself to you in the present scarcity of ammunition. It is one also that may be rendered destructive at night against the enemy at anchor. Even without guns the ship would, it is believed, be formidable as a ram."[67]

"... the Arkansas is very inferior to the Merrimac in every particular. The iron with which she is covered is worn and indifferent, taken from a railroad track, and is poorly secured to the vessel; boiler iron on stern and counter; her smoke-stack is sheet iron."[68]

---

[64] Rodman L. Underwood, *Stephen Russell Mallory: A Biography of the Confederate Navy Secretary and United States Senator* (McFarland, 2005), 38.

[65] J. Thomas Scharf, *History of the Confederate States Navy from Its Organization to the Surrender of Its Last Vessel* (New York: Rogers & Sherwood, 1887), 43.

[66] Ibid., 44.

[67] Ibid., 155.

[68] Ibid., 307.

"A grateful country, while deploring the loss of the gallant dead who fell upon this memorable occasion, will place their names upon the roll of her heroes, and cherish them with respect and affection." [69]

"Against the overwhelming forces brought to bear upon our little squadron defeat seems to have been inevitable; but the bearing of our officers and men has snatched credit even from defeat; and, mingled with deep regret for the suffering and captivity of the brave old admiral and the loss of our men and ships is the conviction that the triumph of the enemy leaves the honor of our service untarnished." [70]

"... should Savannah fall do not permit our vessels under construction or any of the public property in your charge to fall into the hands of the enemy. Destroy everything when necessary to prevent this." [71]

Attorney General (1862-1863)
Thomas Hill Watts

"Gentlemen: On the 11th day of January, 1861, the sovereign people of Alabama, through their delegates in Convention assembled, declared by solemn ordinance, that the bonds which bound her to the Government of the United States were severed. In thus deliberately acting, the people of Alabama only exercised a right belonging to every free people. In the days of 1776, our forefathers declared that to secure life, liberty and the pursuit of happiness, Governments are instituted among men, deriving their powers from the consent of the governed; and that whenever any form of government becomes destructive of these ends, it is the right of the people to altar or abolish it, and to institute new government, laying its foundations on such principles, and organizing its powers in such form as to them shall seem most likely to affect their safety and happiness." [72]

---

[69] Ibid., 322.
[70] Ibid., 581.
[71] Ibid., 650.
[72] *Inaugural Address of Gov. Thomas H. Watts Before the Alabama Legislature, December 1, 1863* (Montgomery: Montgomery Advertiser Book and Job Offices, 1863), 3.

"The simple ordinance of secession declared the Constitution of the United States no longer binding on the people of Alabama; and that they were free to form and adopt a new Constitution to govern them in their relations to other States, and with foreign powers."[73]

"In accordance with the dictates of her judgment, Alabama and other States, now known as the Confederate States of America, formed a new Constitution and a new Government, based on the principles of the old one amending the Constitution so as to leave no room for doubtful construction on disputed points."[74]

"Because of the exercise of this right—a right lying at the foundation of all free government, and the corner stone of every republican system of government, the Northern States, now calling themselves the United States, made war on the Confederate States. The authorities of these Northern States by their declarations and their conduct thus deny the right of free government—deny that all governments derive their powers from the consent of the governed—deny the doctrines of the Declaration of Independence, and the principles of the fathers of the Republic, and assert and attempt to exercise the doctrines of force. They deny to the people of Alabama the right of self government, and declare the monstrous pharisaic dogma, that they have the right to coerce us to be subservient to their will! that they are our superiors our masters! and we, their inferiors! their slaves!"[75]

"The Confederate States were to be forced back into a Union whose first principle was free consent It was vainly imagined by the wisemen of the North that the eighteen millions of Northern whites could and would very soon crush to powder the eight millions of Southern white people; especially as in their vain imaginings they supposed the four millions of blacks were here amongst us ready to burst the bonds which bound them to us. But these men, wise in their own conceit, forgot that 'the battle is not always to the strong, nor the race to the swift.' They forgot that there was a God of justice, the ruler of men and nations."[76]

---

[73] Ibid., 7.
[74] Ibid., 7.
[75] Ibid., 7.
[76] Ibid., 12.

"Our Confederate currency must be upheld. Every dollar's worth of property in the Confederate States is pledged for its redemption. In can only become worthless by our subjugation, by our failure to achieve our independence. If we are ever conquered, we shall conquer ourselves by failure to discharge our duty. If we fail, then nothing we can call our own will be worth a dollar to us. It is the currency which our soldiers receive for their services. If it is good enough for them, it is surely good enough for any property we have. Let it be sustained at all hazards. The credit of the Confederate States is the lifeblood of Southern liberty."[77]

Attorney General (1864-1865)
George Davis

"My public life was long since over; my ambition went down with the banner of the South, and, like it, never rose again. I have had abundant time in all these quiet years, and it has been my favorite occupation to review the occurrences of that time, and recall over the history of that tremendous struggle; to remember with love and admiration the great men who bore their parts in its events."[78]

"I have often thought what was it that the Southern people had to be most proud of in all the proud things of their record? Not the achievements of our arms! No man is more proud of them than I; no man rejoices more in Manassas, Chancellorsville and in Richmond; but all nations have had their victories. There is something, I think, better than that, and it was this, that through all the bitterness of that time, and throughout all the heat of that fierce contest, Jefferson Davis and Robert E. Lee never spoke a word, never wrote a line that the whole neutral world did not accept as the very indisputable truth. Aye, truth was the guiding star of both of them, and that is a grand thing to remember; upon that my memory rests more proudly than upon anything else. It is a monument better than marble, more durable than brass. Teach it to your children, that they may be proud to remember Jefferson Davis."[79]

---

[77] Idid., 20.

[78] *A Memorial of the Hon. George Davis* (Wilmington, N.C., Chamber of Commerce, 1896), 31.

[79] Ibid., 31-32.

"This above all: To thine own self be true, and it must follow as the night the day, thou canst not then be false to any man."[80]

A Representative and a Senator of South Carolina
Robert Barnwell Rhett

"The real issue involved in the relations between the North and the South of the American States, is the great principle of self-government. Shall a dominant party of the North rule the South, or shall the people of the South rule themselves. This is the great matter in controversy."[81]

Senator of Mississippi
Albert Gallatin Brown

"So long as there is a pound of material left, it is our duty to seize it and hurl it at the enemy. Talk of individual rights and the safeguards to liberty, with a million of armed Yankees thundering at your doors. What has become of personal liberty, the habeas corpus, and the written Constitution in Tennessee, Kentucky, Missouri, Arkansas, Mississippi, and wherever else the foe has obtained a footing? Gone, sir; buried deep in the graves that contain the bodies of our slaughtered countrymen; and yet we have exhortations to save these sacred gifts at the peril of losing all that remains to us of our once happy and still beloved country."[82]

"If I cannot save everything, I will save that which is the most valuable. If we lose the country, personal liberty, the habeas corpus, and the Constitution must go with it. We can never wrest these things from Yankee hands if once oar country is conquered. We can, at our own will, take them from the hands of our own chosen rulers. If our jewels are threatened will we allow the enemy to seize them while we are debating whether it is safe to entrust them to the hands of our agents. Mr. President, the blood of our brothers cries to us

---

[80] Ibid., 33.
[81] Robert Barnwell Rhett, *A Fire-eater Remembers: The Confederate Memoir of Robert Barnwell Rhett* (University of South Carolina Press, 2000), 48.
[82] *State of the Country, Speech of Hon. A. G. Brown of Mississippi, In the Confederate Senate* (December 24, 1863), 15.

from the ground. Their disembodied spirits watch over us to-day. They seem to draw nearer and nearer, as we hesitate in the discharge of our duty."[83]

Senator of Texas
Williamson Simpson Oldham

"The people of the North have never failed, when the opportunity was presented, to tender ovations to the most transcendent among the criminals, while their press has been constant in its laudation and their orators and preachers have cried out 'well done.' Army, government and people, have united to make the name of Yankee, suggestive as it was before of fraud, now the synonym of barbarism and baseness."[84]

"Can the bones of our people, scattered over every State of this Confederacy, be gathered together and buried in the tomb of oblivion? Can that gulf between the North and the South, dug by hostile bayonets, wide and deep, extending' from the ocean to the mountains of the west, filled with the reeking blood of our slain martyrs, from which the wailings of our people ever issue forth, and over which the fires of our burning homes are ever blazing, be closed and forever obscured, or converted into a garden yielding the fruits and flowers of peace and safety and, the confidence of fraternal union? Can all these crimes, and ten thousand more against us, against humanity, against God, be forgotten by us, and we, by any means, be induced to live in reunion with the perpetrators of them? The resolves just read, answers for my State: 'By the just pride of the manhood and the virtue which we claim as individuals, and as a people; by the divine command which warns us not to walk in the way of the wicked; by the memory of our murdered dead; by the sight of bereaved mothers, widows, sisters, daughters, and orphans in our land; by the heart-brokenness of trampled virtue, and by our desolated hearths, we are forbidden to admit a thought of further association with the people of the North. Our heroic soldiers, the living and the martyred dead, forbid it I and our trust in God forbids it!'"[85]

---

[83] Ibid., 15-16.

[84] *Speech of Hon. W. S. Oldham, of Texas on the Resolutions of the State of Texas, Concerning Peace, Reconstruction and Independence In the Confederate States Senate* (January 30, 1865), 2.

[85] Ibid., 2.

"Better to die ten thousand deaths than to live in such a union, of wrong, of hate, of scorn, of shame, of infamy and degradation! Better that the earth should open and swallow us up, with our country, our wives and children, and all that we have, obliterating our name and race from amongst the living, than for us to submit to such a reunion!"[86]

"Our enemies tender us this reunion as the only terms of peace, and threaten us, in case of refusal, with all the horrors of subjugation. Subjugation! What does it mean? Bo Senators, do our people, comprehend what it means? It means the erasing of our name and country from the map of the world; the conclusion of our history, with no future; the destruction of our governments, both State and Confederate, and the provincializing of our States, to be governed by a triumvirate, consisting of the whining, canting, hypocritical Yankee ... It means Yankee governors to rule us, Yankee legislators to make our laws, Yankee judges to expound and administer them, and Yankee ministerial officers to enforce and carry them into execution. It means the confiscation of our property to pay their national debt, contracted for our subjugation, the death of our leading citizens, by military executions, or otherwise, for having defended their country and its liberties against their invaders. It means the crushing of the heart by the buffetings and scorn, chastisement and contempt, of the living, and the outrage and violation of their mothers, sisters, wives, and daughters, by a brutalized negro soldiery, stationed in every town and city and quartered in the houses of the people, to keep them in subjection and crush out the spirit of liberty."[87]

"Senators, let us arouse ourselves from our lethargy, and quickly, but wisely, discharge our duties here ; then let us go to our brave sons in the army and speak the words of confidence and courage to them. Thank God, they need them not; but, after four years of toil, service, and battle, they are sending those words to us. Then let us go to our people at home, and cheer and arouse them from any depression of spirit that may oppress them, 'instruct their minds, and fire their hearts' with enthusiastic devotion to their country's cause, and nerve their arms to 'Strike for our altar and our fires, strike for the green grave of our sires; Strike till the last armed foe expires, For God and our native land.'"[88]

---

[86] Ibid., 12.
[87] Ibid., 12-13.
[88] Ibid., 13.

Senator of Tennessee
Gustavus Adolphus Henry

"On these principles our fathers, more than eighty years ago, though comparatively few in numbers, grappled with the power of Great Britain, and, after seven years of war, in which their country was desolated, and their cities occupied, possessed and sacked by the enemy, finally triumphed. On these same principles we have staked our all, in the war in which we are engaged with the United States; and though our country may be despoiled and ravaged, our cities given to the flames, and nothing be left but the 'blackness of ashes' to mark where they stood, we, too, will finally triumph and achieve our independence."[89]

"In 1787, when they formed the Constitution of the United States, they met as equal sovereignties. They did not afterwards sink their separate State sovereignty, abolish their State governments, and have one legislature, as in the ease of England, Ireland, and Scotland. No, sir. They maintained their State sovereignty, in opposition to centralism, as being the great enemy of liberty in free States, which would swallow them in the whirlpool of consolidation, but for the spirit of local self-governments, always the life-blood of freedom."[90]

"Mr. President, we have now maintained this unequal contest for nearly four years, and invoke the judgment of the world whether or not we have established our capacity for self-government, and our ability to resist the power of the enemy to subjugate us."[91]

"We need but look to the present and the past, to settle the question of our ability to resist the power of the enemy. Less than four years ago we were without an army and navy. Our enemy took possession of both, and turned them against us. The wealth of the country was at the North; and the pernicious system of legislation pursued so long and so persistingly to our prejudice and to the aggrandizement of the North, had concentrated there

---

[89] *Speech of Hon. Gustavus A. Henry of Tennessee, in the Senate of the Confederate States* (November 29, 1864), 2.
[90] Ibid., 3.
[91] Ibid., 5.

nearly all the public works and manufacturing power of the whole country. We had neither heavy ordnance nor small arms; manufactured neither ponder nor ball; not even percussion caps. But see the progress we have made, and how we have developed our resources."[92]

"We have met the enemy in a hundred battles, and have baffled and defeated his armies in conflicts without number on the land, and our little navy has nearly driven his commerce from the seas. We have struck the world with astonishment at the power we have exhibited, while the gaze of all Europe is fixed in admiration of the gallantry of our soldier. If we consider our small and meagre resources at the beginning, and the material strength we wield now, we are ourselves astonished at the progress we have made in the art of war and the science of government."[93]

"If we were to agree to, go into a convention of the States, we would be bound, on honor, to abide its decision. They outnumber us two to one, and, of course, would have us in their power. We would deliver ourselves over to them, bound hand and foot, to receive the scourge which their malice would inflict, and which our fatuity and folly would richly merit. No, sir; let our enemy know, and let the world bear witness, we strike for independence and will be satisfied with nothing else. Reunion with the United States would result in bondage to us. The bondage under which Ireland groans—the tyranny which England has, for so many years, inflicted upon that down-trodden people, would be visited upon us by our enemies. Death would be infinitely preferable to such a condition."[94]

"Reunion with them? No, sir; never! There is a great gulf that rolls between us. It is a gulf of blood, without a shore and without a bottom, and is as impassable as that which separates Dives from Lazarus. The mute objects of nature; our desecrated churches and altars; our sweet valleys drenched in blood and charred by fire, forbid it. The dead would cry out against it from their gory beds. The blood of my own sons, yet unavenged, cries to Heaven from the ground for vengeance. The thousands who are sleeping red in their graves would awake and utter their solemn protest. Stonewall Jackson,

---

[92] Ibid., 5.
[93] Ibid., 6.
[94] Ibid., 6.

Polk, Stuart, Rodes, Morgan, Preston Smith, and the thousands over whose remains a monument to the unknown dead shall be raised, are speaking in tones of thunder against it; and can it be the living only will be dumb? Sir, those who have died in this war are not dead to us. 'E'en in their ashes live their wonted fires.'"[95]

"If it be the purpose of the enemy to prolong the war, let us begin anew to prepare for it. When mast after mast on Paul Jones' vessel was carried away by the cannon balls of the enemy, till not one was left standing, and that enemy had boarded his vessel, and he was called upon to surrender, he heroically shouted aloud, 'I will never surrender; I am just getting ready to fight.' Let us emulate the example of that stout-hearted sailor. The Government should organize its strength, and, especially, execute our laws. The failure to do so stamps weakness on all our efforts to fill the army. Let us prepare in earnest for the defence of our country, and give cordially every power to the Government that is necessary to establish our independence."[96]

Senator of Alabama
William L. Yancey

"Mr. President, I do not believe we are weakened for war by too much constitutional liberty. I have full faith in this complicated and limited Government to carry us safely through this war. Its strength, however, lies in the most careful observance of the rights of each department of the Government and of each State. Its greatest weakness is in a disposition to assume powers from a mischievous and fallacious idea that they are necessary to our safety. Such assumption is more to be feared, more dangerous, in my opinion, than are a million of Yankee bayonets. Let there be mutual respect fur the rights of each and all—and there will result a harmony and an energy and a power that will secure to us all we value in constitutional government."[97]

---

[95] Ibid., 7.
[96] Ibid., 8.
[97] *Speeches of William L. Yancey, Esq., Senator From the State of Alabama Made in the Senate of the Confederate States During the Session Commencing On the 18th day of August, A.D. 1862* (Montgomery Advertiser Book and Job Office, 1862), 41.

"It should also be borne in mind, that our enemy does not admit that we have a rightful government, either State or Confederate, deeming and treating our system of governments but as so many rebellious organizations, and their war, therefore, is both in theory and in practice waged against each loyal citizen of the Confederacy as a rebel."[98]

---

[98] Ibid., 5-6.

Soldiers of the Confederacy

Robert Edward Lee
Thomas Jonathan Jackson
James Ewell Brown Stuart
Albert Sidney Johnston
Patrick Ronayne Cleburne
John Bell Hood
Wade Hampton
Nathan Bedford Forrest
Albert Pike
Edmund Kirby-Smith
George Edward Pickett
Pierre Gustave Toutant Beauregard
John Hunt Morgan
John Singleton Mosby
Joseph Wheeler

Edward Porter Alexander
Carlton McCarthy
John Daniel Imboden
John Pelham
Lewis A. Armistead
Robert Lewis Dabney
Robert Tansil
Roger Weightman Hanson
Sam R. Watkins
Eli Pinson Landers
Reuben Everett Wilson
Benjamin McCulloch
Barnard Bee
Daniel Harvey Hill
Alfred Marmaduke Hobby

"All the South has ever desired was that the Union, as established by our forefathers, should be preserved and that the government, as originally organized, should be administered in purity and truth."[99]

Robert E. Lee

General in Chief of the Armies of the Confederate States
Robert Edward Lee

"Duty, then, is the sublimest word in our language. Do your duty in all things, like the old Puritan. You cannot do more; you should never wish to do less."[100]

"I cannot consent to place in the control of others one who cannot control himself."[101]

"There is nothing left for me to do but to go and see General Grant and I would rather die a thousand deaths."[102]

"'I would have preferred that your choice had fallen upon an abler man. Trusting in Almighty God, a good conscience, and the aid of my fellow-citizens, I devote myself to the service of my native State, in whose behalf alone will I ever again draw my sword."[103]

---

[99] J. William Jones, *Personal Reminiscences, Anecdotes, and Letters of General Robert E. Lee* (New York: D. Appleton & Company, 1874), 210.

[100] Thomas Nelson Page, *Robert E. Lee: The Southerner* (New York: Charles Scribner's Sons, 1908), 29.

[101] J. William Jones, *Personal Reminiscences, Anecdotes, and Letters of General Robert E. Lee* (New York: D. Appleton & Company, 1874), 170.

[102] Mary L. Williamson, *Life of Robert E. Lee* (Richmond: Johnson Publishing Company, 1918), 102-103.

[103] Thomas Nelson Page, *Robert E. Lee: Man and Soldier* (New York: Charles Scribner's Sons, 1911), 81-82.

"We are conscious that we have humbly tried to do our duty, we may, therefore, with calm satisfaction trust in God and leave results to Him."[104]

"Relying upon your judgment, courage, and discretion, and trusting to the continued blessing of an ever-kind Providence, I hope for victory."[105]

"It is well that war is so terrible, otherwise we should grow too fond of it."[106]

"I have been up to see the Congress and they do not seem to be able to do anything except to eat peanuts and chew tobacco, while my army is starving."[107]

"Never do a wrong thing to make a friend or to keep one."[108]

"The education of a man or woman is never completed till they die."[109]

"In a letter to Hon. A. W. Beresford Hope, acknowledging the receipt of a Bible from friends in England, he speaks of it as 'a book, in comparison with which all others in my eyes are of minor importance; and which in all my perplexities and distresses has never failed to give me light and strength.'"[110]

"Read history, works of truth, not novels, and romances. Get correct views of life and learn to see the world in its true light."[111]

---

[104] Thomas Nelson Page, *Robert E. Lee: Man and Soldier* (New York: Charles Scribner's Sons, 1911), 65.

[105] Henry Alexander White, *Robert E. Lee and the Southern Confederacy, 1807-1870* (New York: G.P. Putman's Sons, 1897), 175.

[106] Fitzhugh Lee, *General Lee* (New York: D. Appleton & Company, 1913), 294.

[107] C. Brian Kelly, *Best Little Ironies, Oddities, and Mysteries of the Civil War* (Cumberland House Publishing, 2000), 296.

[108] Henry Alexander White, *Robert E. Lee and the Southern Confederacy, 1807-1870* (New York: G.P. Putman's Sons, 1897), 49.

[109] J. William Jones, *Life and Letters of Robert Edward Lee, Soldier and Man* (New York: The Neale Publishing Company, 1906), 117.

[110] Ibid., 470.

[111] Franklin L. Riley, *General Robert E. Lee after Appomattox* (New York: MacMillian Company, 1922), 160.

"There is a true glory and a true honor: the glory of duty done — the honor of the integrity of principle."[112]

"My trust is in the mercy and wisdom of a kind Providence, who ordereth all things for our good."[113]

"Obedience to lawful authority is the foundation of manly character."[114]

"I need to tell you that true patriotism sometimes requires of men to act exactly contrary, at one period, to that which it does at another, and the motive which impels them the desire to do right is precisely the same."[115]

"Go home all you boys who fought with me and help build up the shattered fortunes of our old state"[116]

"Cadets can neither be treated as schoolboys or soldiers."[117]

"I have fought against the people of North because I believed they were seeking to wrest from the South its dearest rights. But I have never cherished toward them bitter or vindictive feelings, and I have never seen the day I did not pray for them."[118]

"I can only say that I am nothing but a poor sinner, trusting in Christ alone for salvation."[119]

---

[112] J. G. DeRoulhac Hamilton and Mary Thompson Hamilton, *The Life of Robert E. Lee for Boys and Girls* (Houghton Mifflin Company, 1917), 105.
[113] Iain C. Martin, *The Quotable American Civil War* (Lyons Press, 2008), 209.
[114] H.W. Crocker III, *Robert E. Lee on Leadership: Executive Lessons in Character, Courage, and Vision* (Random House, 2010), 172.
[115] J. William Jones, *Personal Reminiscences, Anecdotes, and Letters of General Robert E. Lee* (New York: D. Appleton & Company, 1874), 208.
[116] Noah Andre Trudeau, *Robert E. Lee* (MacMillan, 2009), 202.
[117] Emory M. Thomas, *Robert E. Lee: A Biography* (W. W. Norton & Company, 1997), 157.
[118] A. L. Long, *Memoirs of Robert E. Lee: His Military and Personal History* (J. M. Stoddart & Company, 1887), 484-485.
[119] Theodore L. Flood and Frank Chapin Bray, *The Chautauquan, Volume 31* (1900), 188.

"It is easier to make our wishes conform to our means than to make our means conform to our wishes."[120]

"What a cruel thing is war: to separate and destroy families and friends, and mar the purest joys and happiness God has granted us in this world; to fill our hearts with hatred instead of love for our neighbors, and to devastate the fair face of this beautiful world. I pray that, on this day when only peace and good-will are preached to mankind, better thoughts may fill the hearts of our enemies and turn them to peace."[121]

"A true man of honor feels humbled himself when he cannot help humbling others."[122]

"My trust is in the mercy and wisdom of a kind Providence, who ordereth all things for our good."[123]

"Obedience to lawful authority is the foundation of manly character."[124]

"We all thought Richmond, protected as it was by our splendid fortifications and defended by our army of veterans, could not be taken. Yet Grant turned his face to our Capital, and never turned it away until we had surrendered. Now, I have carefully searched the military records of both ancient and modern history, and have never found Grant's superior as a general. I doubt that his superior can be found in all history."[125]

"If Virginia stands by the old Union, so will I. But if she secedes ... then I will still follow my native state with my sword and if need be with my life."[126]

---

[120] J. William Jones, *Personal Reminiscences, Anecdotes, and Letters of General Robert E. Lee* (New York: D. Appleton & Company, 1874), 281.
[121] Robert Edward Lee, *Robert E. Lee Softer Side* (Pelican Publishing, 2007), 102.
[122] Michael Fellman, *The Making of Robert E. Lee* (JHU Press, 2003), 8.
[123] Iain C. Martin, *The Quotable American Civil War* (Lyons Press, 2008), 209.
[124] Richard G. Williams, Jr., *Maxims of Robert E. Lee for Young Gentlemen* (Pelican Publishing, 2005), 57.
[125] *Report of the Proceedings of the Reunions of the Society of the Army of the Tennessee, Volume 33* (Society of the Army of the Tennessee, 1902), 98.
[126] Alan T. Nolan, *Lee Considered: General Robert E. Lee and Civil War History*

"If we can defeat or drive the armies of the enemy from the field, we shall have peace, all our effort and energies should be devoted to that object."[127]

"With all my devotion to the Union and the feeling of loyalty and duty of an American citizen I have not been able to make up my mind to raise my hand against my relatives, my children, my home."[128]

"When a man makes a mistake, I call him into my tent, talk to him, and use the authority of my position to make him do the right thing the next time"[129]

"We cannot afford to be idle, and though weaker than our opponents in men and military equipments, must endeavor to harass, if we cannot destroy them."[130]

"I think and work with all my powers to bring my troops to the right place at the right time; then I have done my duty, then I leave the matter up to God and the subordinate officers."[131]

"My father was the most punctual man I ever knew…He used to appear some minutes before the rest of us, in uniform, jokingly rallying my mother for being late, and for forgetting something at the last moment. When he could wait no longer for her, he would say he was off and would march along to church by himself."[132]

(UNC Press Books, 1996), 36.

[127] Elizabeth Brown Pryor, *Reading the Man – A Portrait of Robert E. Lee Through His Private Letters* (New York: Penguin Group, 2007), 285.

[128] J. William Jones, *Personal Reminiscences, Anecdotes, and Letters of General Robert E. Lee* (New York: D. Appleton & Company, 1874), 139.

[129] Emory M. Thomas, *Robert E. Lee: A Biography* (W. W. Norton & Company, 1997), 332.

[130] Jeffry D. Wert, *Cavalryman of the Lost Cause: A Biography of J. E. B. Stuart* (Simon and Schuster, 2009), 139.

[131] John David Smith, Thomas H. Appleton, Charles Pierce Roland, *A Mythic Land Apart: Reassessing Southerners and Their History* (Greenwood Publishing Group, 1997), 113.

[132] Robert Edward Lee, *Recollections and Letters of General Robert E. Lee* (Doubleday, Page & Company, 1904), 12.

"We could have pursued no other course without dishonor. And as sad as the results have been, if it had all to be done over again, we should be compelled to act in precisely the same manner."[133]

"There is no more dangerous experiment than that of undertaking to be one thing before a man's face and another behind his back."[134]

"You must study to be frank with the world: frankness is the child of honesty and courage. Say just what you mean to do on every occasion, and take it for granted that you mean to do right."[135]

"My experience through life has convinced me that, while moderation and temperance in all things are commendable and beneficial, abstinence from spirituous liquors is the best safeguard of morals and health"[136]

"The gentleman does not needlessly and unnecessarily remind an offender of a wrong he may have committed against him. He can not only forgive; he can forget; and he strives for that nobleness of self and mildness of character which imparts sufficient strength to let the past be put the past."[137]

"We failed, but in the good providence of God apparent failure often proves a blessing."[138]

"Get correct views of life, and learn to see the world in its true light. It will enable you to live pleasantly, to do good, and, when summoned away, to leave without regret."[139]

---

[133] James Ronald Kennedy, *The South was Right!* (Pelican Publishing, 1994), 155.

[134] A. L. Long, *Memoirs of Robert E. Lee: His Military and Personal History* (J. M. Stoddart & Company, 1887), 484-485.

[135] Judith White McGuire, *General Robert E. Lee, the Christian Soldier* (Claxton, Remsen & Haffelfinger, 1873), 59.

[136] J. William Jones, *Personal Reminiscences, Anecdotes, and Letters of General Robert E. Lee* (New York: D. Appleton & Company, 1874), 153.

[137] Emory M. Thomas, *Robert E. Lee: A Biography* (W. W. Norton & Company, 1997), 397.

[138] H.W. Crocker III, *Robert E. Lee on Leadership: Executive Lessons in Character, Courage, and Vision* (Random House, 2010), 176.

[139] Robert Edward Lee, *Recollections and Letters of General Robert E. Lee*

"I am of the opinion that all who can should vote for the most intelligent, honest, and conscientious men eligible to office, irrespective of former party opinions, who will endeavour to make the new constitutions and the laws passed under them as beneficial as possible to the true interests, prosperity, and liberty of all classes and conditions of the people."[140]

"Still a Union that can only be maintained by swords and bayonets, and in which strife and civil war are to take the place of brotherly love and kindness, has no charm for me."[141]

"My experiences of men has neither disposed me to think worse of them nor be indisposed to serve them: nor, in spite of failures which I lament, of errors which I now see and acknowledge, or the present aspect of affairs, do I despair of the future. The truth is this: The march of Providence is so slow and our desires so impatient; the work of progress so immense and our means of aiding it so feeble; the life of humanity is so long, that of the individual so brief, that we often see only the ebb of the advancing wave and are thus discouraged. It is history that teaches us to hope."[142]

"Private and public life are subject to the same rules; and truth and manliness are two qualities that will carry you through this world much better than policy, or tact, or expediency, or any other word that was ever devised to conceal or mystify a deviation from the straight line."[143]

"We have fought this fight as long, and as well as we know how. We have been defeated. For us as a Christian people, there is now but one course to pursue. We must accept the situation."[144]

(Doubleday, Page & Company, 1904), 248.

[140] J. William Jones, *Personal Reminiscences, Anecdotes, and Letters of General Robert E. Lee* (New York: D. Appleton & Company, 1874), 228.

[141] *Lee Considered: General Robert E. Lee and Civil War History* (UNC Press Books, 1996), 35.

[142] R. A. Brock, *Southern Historical Society Papers, Volume 17* (Richmond: Published by the Society, 1876), 245.

[143] J. William Jones, *Life and Letters of Robert Edward Lee, Soldier and Man* (New York: The Neale Publishing Company, 1906), 439.

[144] Philip Alexander Bruce, *Robert E. Lee* (G.W. Jacobs, 1907), 307.

"My chief concern is to try to be a humble, earnest Christian"[145]

"God's will ought to be our aim, and I am quite content that His designs should be accomplished and not mine."[146]

"We are all in the hands of a kind God, who will do for us what is best, and more than we deserve ... May we all deserve His mercy, His care, and His protection."[147]

"I prefer the Bible to any other book. There is enough in that to satisfy the most ardent thirst for knowledge; to open the way to true wisdom; and to teach the only road to salvation and eternal happiness. It is not above human comprehension, and is sufficient to satisfy all its desires... I accept it as the infallible Word of God and receive its teachings as inspired by the Holy Ghost."[148]

"That it maybe so, listen to the teachings of your parents, obey their percepts and from childhood to the grave pursue unswervingly the paths of honor and of truth. Above all things, learn at once to worship your Creator and to do His will as revealed in His Holy Book."[149]

"God disposes. This ought to satisfy us."[150]

"Honesty in its widest sense is always admirable. The trite saying that Honesty is the best policy has met with the just criticism that honesty is not

---

[145] J. Steven Wilkins, *Call of Duty: The Sterling Nobility of Robert E. Lee* (Cumberland House Publishing, 1997), 183.

[146] J. William Jones, *Personal Reminiscences, Anecdotes, and Letters of General Robert E. Lee* (New York: D. Appleton & Company, 1874), 143.

[147] Carl Coke Rister, *Robert E. Lee in Texas* (University of Oklahoma Press, 1946), 60.

[148] Marshall L. DeRosa, *The Enduring Relevance of Robert E. Lee: The Ideological Warfare Underpinning the American Civil War* (Lexington Books, 2013), 72.

[149] J. William Jones, *Personal Reminiscences, Anecdotes, and Letters of General Robert E. Lee* (New York: D. Appleton & Company, 1874), 411.

[150] A. L. Long, *Memoirs of Robert E. Lee: His Military and Personal History* (J. M. Stoddart & Company, 1887), 485.

policy. This seems to be true. The real honest man is honest from conviction of what is right, not from policy."[151]

"Those who oppose our purposes are not always to be regarded as our enemies. We usually think and act from our immediate surroundings."[152]

"The better rule is to judge our adversaries from their standpoint, not from ours."[153]

"Fame which does not result from good actions and achievements for the good of the whole people is not to be desired."[154]

"No man can be so important in the world that he needs not the good-will and approval of others."[155]

"Charity should have no beginning or ending."[156]

"Soldiers! we have sinned against Almighty God. We have forgotten His signal mercies, and have cultivated a revengeful, haughty, and boastful spirit. We have not remembered that the defenders of a just cause should be pure in His eyes; that our times are in His hands, and we have relied too much on our own arms for the achievement of our independence. God is our only refuge and our strength. Let us humble ourselves before Him. Let us confess our many sins and beseech Him to give us a higher courage, a purer patriotism, and a more determined will; that He will convert the hearts of our enemies; that He will hasten the time when war, with its sorrows and

---

[151] Ibid., 485.

[152] Thomas Nelson Page, *The Works of Thomas Nelson Page, Volume 18* (C. Scribner's Sons, 1912), 361.

[153] A. L. Long, *Memoirs of Robert E. Lee: His Military and Personal History* (J. M. Stoddart & Company, 1887), 485.

[154] Richard G. Williams, Jr., *Maxims of Robert E. Lee for Young Gentle* (Pelican Publishing, 2005), 21.

[155] J. Steven Wilkins, *Call of Duty: The Sterling Nobility of Robert E. Lee* (Cumberland House Publishing, 1997), 148.

[156] Thomas Nelson Page, *The Works of Thomas Nelson Page, Volume 18* (C. Scribner's Sons, 1912), 361.

sufferings, shall cease, and that He will give us a name and place among the nations of the earth."[157]

"We must expect reverses, even defeats. They are sent to teach us wisdom and prudence, to call forth greater energies, and to prevent our falling into greater disasters."[158]

"No human power can avail us without the blessing of God and I rejoice to know that, in this crisis of our affairs, good men everywhere are supplicating Him for His favor and protection."[159]

"I dread the thought of any student going away from the college without becoming a sincere Christian."[160]

"I think it better to do right, even if we suffer in so doing, than to incur the reproach of our consciences and posterity."[161]

"Governor, if I had foreseen the use those people designed to make of their victory, there would have been no surrender at Appomattox Courthouse; no sir, not by me. Had I foreseen these results of subjugation, I would have preferred to die at Appomattox with my brave men, my sword in this right hand."[162]

"The reputation of individuals is of minor importance to the opinion which posterity may form of the motives which governed the South in their late struggle for the maintenance of the principles of the Constitution. I hope, therefore, a true history will be written and justice be done them."[163]

---

[157] James Dabney McCabe, *Life and Campaigns of General Robert E. Lee* (National Publishing Company, 1866), 413.

[158] Michael Fellman, *The Making of Robert E. Lee* (JHU Press, 2003), 151.

[159] J. William Jones, *Personal Reminiscences, Anecdotes, and Letters of General Robert E. Lee* (New York: D. Appleton & Company, 1874), 411.

[160] Franklin Lafayette Riley, *General Robert E. Lee After Appomattox* (Macmillan Company, 1922), 193.

[161] Walter Brian Cisco, Wade Hampton (Potomac Books, Inc., 2004), 129.

[162] Thomas Carry Johnson, *Life and Letters of Robert Lewis Dabney* (Richmond : The Presbyterian Committee of Publications, 1903), 499-500.

[163] A. L. Long, *Memoirs of Robert E. Lee: His Military and Personal History* (J. M. Stoddart & Company, 1887), 4.

"Is it not strange that the descendants of those Pilgrim Fathers who crossed the Atlantic to preserve the freedom of their opinion have always proved themselves intolerant of the spiritual liberty of others."[164]

"I fought against the people of the North because they were seeking to wrest from the South it's dearest rights. But I have never cherished toward them bitter or vindictive feelings, and I have never seen the day when I did not pray for them."[165]

"We had, I was satisfied, sacred principles to maintain and rights to defend for which we were in duty bound to do our best, even if we perished in the endeavor."[166]

Lieutenant General Thomas Jonathan "Stonewall" Jackson

"Captain, my religious belief teaches me to feel as safe in battle as in bed. God has fixed the time for my death. I do not concern myself about that, but to be always ready, no matter when it may overtake me." He added, after a pause, looking me full in the face: "That is the way all men should live, and then all would be equally brave"[167]

"Should the steps be taken which is now threatened, we shall have no other alternative: we must fight. But do not think that all Christian people of the land could be induced to unite in prayer, to avert so great an evil. It seems to me that if they would unite in prayer, war might be prevented and peace preserved."[168]

---

[164] Fitzhugh Lee, *General Lee* (New York: D. Appleton and Company, 1898), 64.

[165] J. William Jones, *Personal Reminiscences, Anecdotes, and Letters of General Robert E. Lee* (New York: D. Appleton & Company, 1874), 196.

[166] J. G. DeRoulhac Hamilton and Mary Thompson Hamilton, *The Life of Robert E. Lee for Boys and Girls* (Houghton Mifflin Company, 1917), 104.

[167] G. F. R. Henderson, *Stonewall Jackson and the American Civil War, Vol. 1* (Longmans, Green, and Co., 1909), 163.

[168] Henry Alexander White, *Stonewall Jackson* (G. W. Jacobs, 1909), 67.

"The only true rule for cavalry is to follow the enemy as long as he retreats."[169]

"I am more anxious than I can tell that my men shall be good soldiers of the cross as well as good soldiers of their country."[170]

"Always mystify, mislead, and surprise the enemy, if possible; and when you strike and overcome him, never let up in the pursuit so long as your men have strength to follow; for an army routed, if hotly pursued, becomes panic-stricken, and can then be destroyed by half their number."[171]

"Yesterday we fought a great battle and gained a great victory, for which all the glory is due to God alone. Although under a heavy fire for several continuous hours I received only one wound, the breaking of the longest finger of my left hand; but the doctor says the finger may be saved. It was broken about midway between the hand and knuckle, the ball passing on the side next to the forefinger. Had it struck the centre, I should have lost the finger. My horse was wounded, but not killed. Your coat got an ugly wound near the hip, but my servant, who is very handy, has so far repaired it that it doesn't show very much. My preservation was entirely due, as was the glorious victory, to our God, to whom be all the honor, praise, and glory. The battle was the hardest that I have ever been in, but not near so hot in its fire."[172]

"My dear pastor, in my tent last night, after a fatiguing day's service, I remembered that I failed to send a contribution for our colored Sunday School. Enclosed you will find a check for that object, which please acknowledge at your earliest convenience and oblige yours faithfully."[173]

---

[169] George Francis Robert Henderson, *Stonewall Jackson and the American Civil War, Vol. 1* (New York: Longmans, Green & Company, 1909), 392.

[170] Mary Anna Jackson, *Memoirs of Stonewall Jackson* (Louisville: The Prentice Press, 1895), 480.

[171] Henry Alexander White, *Stonewall Jackson* (G.W. Jacobs, 1909), 187.

[172] Mary Anna Jackson, *Memoirs of Stonewall Jackson* (Louisville: The Prentice Press, 1895), 177-178.

[173] Joseph Brummell Earnest, *The Religious Development of the Negro in Virginia* (Charlottesville, Virginia: The Michie Company, Printers, 1914), 84.

"Nothing justifies profanity."[174]

"In the Army of the Shenandoah, you were the First Brigade! In the Army of the Potomac you were the First Brigade! In the Second Corps of this Army, you are the First Brigade! You are the First Brigade in the affections of your general, and I hope by your future deeds and bearing you will be handed down the posterity as the First Brigade in this our Second War of Independence. Farewell!"[175]

"Our men fought bravely but the superior numbers of the enemy repulsed me. Many valuable lives were lost. Our God was my shield. His protecting care is an additional cause for gratitude."[176]

"I yield to no man in sympathy for the gallant men under my command; but I am obliged to sweat them tonight, so that I may save their blood tomorrow."[177]

"Major, my men have sometimes failed to take a position, but to defend one, never!"[178]

"I see from the number of physicians that you think my condition dangerous, but I thank God, if it is His will, that I am ready to go."[179]

"No, sir, I cannot do it. I tell you I am more afraid of King Alcohol than of all the bullets of the enemy."[180]

---

[174] Robert Christy, *Proverbs, Maxims and Phrases of All Ages Volume 1* (New York: C. P. Putnam's Sons, 1888), 167.

[175] John Esten Cooke, Moses Drury Hoge, John William Jones, *Stonewall Jackson: A Military Biography* (New York: A. Appleton and Company, 1876), 85-86.

[176] Henry Alexander White, *Stonewall Jackson* (G.W. Jacobs, 1909), 124.

[177] Ethan Sepp Rafuse, *Stonewall Jackson: A Biography* (ABC-CLIO, 2011), 90.

[178] Donald A. Davis, *Stonewall Jackson* (Palgrave Macmillan, 2007), 170.

[179] John Esten Cooke, Moses Drury Hoge, John William Jones, *Stonewall Jackson: A Military Biography* (New York: A. Appleton and Company, 1876), 484.

[180] J. William Jones, *Personal Reminiscences, Anecdotes, and Letters of General Robert E. Lee* (New York: D. Appleton & Company, 1874), 171.

"War means fighting; to fight is the duty of the soldier; march swiftly, strike the foe with all your strength and take away from him everything you can. Inquire him in every possible way, and do it quickly." [181]

"War means fighting. The business of the soldier is to fight. Armies are not called out to dig trenches, to throw up breastworks, and live in camps, but to find the enemy and strike him; to invade his country, and do him all possible damage in the shortest possible time." [182]

"Such a war would of necessity be of brief countenance, and so would be an economy of prosperity and life in the end. To move swiftly, strike vigorously, and secure all the fruit's of victory is the secret of successful war." [183]

"Throughout the broad extent of country over which you have marched, by your respect for the rights and the property of citizens, you have shown that you were soldiers, not only to defend, but able and willing both to defend and protect." [184]

"Once you get them running, you stay right on top of them, and that way a small force can defeat a large one every time." [185]

"We must make this campaign an exceedingly active one. Only thus can a weaker country cope with a stronger. It must make up in activity, what it lacks in strength, and a defensive campaign can only be made successful by taking the aggressive at the proper time. Don't wait for the adversary to be fully prepared, but strike him the first blow." [186]

---

[181] William C. Chase, *Story of Stonewall Jackson: A Narrative of the Career of Thomas Jonathan (Stonewall) Jackson, from Written and Verbal Accounts of His Life* (D. E. Luther Publishing Company, 1901), 461.

[182] Ethan Sepp Rafuse, *Stonewall Jackson: A Biography* (ABC-CLIO, 2011), 76.

[183] Ibid., 76.

[184] Stonewall Jackson, *The life of Stonewall Jackson: From Official Papers, Contemporary Narratives, and Personal Acquaintance* (New York: Charles B. Richardson, 1864), 34.

[185] Geoffrey C. Ward, *The Civil War* (Random House LLC, 1994), 234.

[186] Elihu Samuel Riley, *Stonewall Jackson: A Thesaurus of Ancedotes of and Incidents in the Life of Lieut. General Jonathan Jackson, C.S.A.* (Elihu Samuel Riley, 1920), 155.

"I like liquor — its taste and its effects — and that is just the reason why I never drink it."[187]

"Through life let your principal object be the discharge of duty. Disregard public opinion when it interferes with your duty. Endeavor to be at peace with all men. Sacrifice your life rather than your word. Endeavor to do well with everything you undertake. Never speak disrespectfully of anyone without a cause. Spare no effort to suppress selfishness, unless that effort would entail sorrow. Let your conduct towards men have some uniformity."[188]

"The patriot volunteer, fighting for country and his rights, makes the most reliable soldier on earth."[189]

"If the general government should persist in the measures now threatened, there must be war. It is painful to discover with what unconcern they speak of war, and threaten it. They do not know its horrors. I have seen enough of it to make me look upon it as the sum of all evils."[190]

"Let us cross over the river, and rest under the shade of the trees."[191]

"It was a sad work; but I had my orders, and my duty was to obey. If the cost of the property could only have been expended in disseminating the gospel of the Prince of peace, how much good might have been expected!"[192]

"I have been officially informed of my promotion to be a Brigadier-General of the Provisional Army of the Southern Confederacy. My promotion is beyond what I anticipated, as I only expected it to be in the volunteer forces

---

[187] J. William Jones, *Personal Reminiscences, Anecdotes, and Letters of General Robert E. Lee* (New York: D. Appleton & Company, 1874), 154.

[188] William C. Chase, *Story of Stonewall Jackson: A Narrative of the Career of Thomas Jonathan (Stonewall) Jackson, from Written and Verbal Accounts of His Life* (D. E. Luther Publishing Company, 1901), 102.

[189] Ibid., 257.

[190] Mary Anna Jackson, *Life and letters of General Thomas J. Jackson* (Harper & Brothers, 1892), 141.

[191] Ibid., 471.

[192] Robert Lewis Dabney, *Life and Campaigns of Lieut.-Gen. Thomas J. Jackson* (Blelock & Company, 1866), 201.

of the State. One of the greatest [grounds of] desires for advancement is the gratification it will give you, and serving my country more efficiently. Through the blessing of God I now have all that I ought to desire in the line of promotion. I would be very ungrateful if I were not contented, and exceedingly thankful to our kind heavenly Father. May his blessing ever rest on you, is my fervent prayer!"[193]

"I had rather lose one man in marching than five in fighting."[194]

"... the hardships of forced marches are often more painful than the dangers of battle."[195]

"If we cannot be successful in defeating the enemy should he advance, a kind Providence may enable us to inflict a terrible wound and affect a safe retreat in the event of having to fall back."[196]

"If officers desire to have control over their commands, they must remain habitually with them, industriously attend to their instruction and comfort, and in battle lead them well and in battle lead them well, and in such a manner as to command their admiration."[197]

"Now, gentlemen, let us at once to bed, and see if tomorrow we cannot do something."[198]

---

[193] Ibid., 204-205.

[194] G. F. E. Henderson, *Stonewall Jackson and the American Civil War, Volume 1* (New York: Longmans, Green and Company, 1909), 427.

[195] William Allan, *Stonewall Jackson, Robert E. Lee, and the Army of Northern Virginia, 1862* (Da Capo Press, 1880), 124.

[196] Elihu Samuel Riley, *Stonewall Jackson: A Thesaurus of Ancedotes of and Incidents in the Life of Lieut. General Jonathan Jackson, C.S.A.* (Elihu Samuel Riley, 1920), 40.

[197] William Allan, *History of the campaign of Gen. T.J. (Stonewall) Jackson in the Shenandoah Valley of Virginia* (Philadelphia: J. B. Lippincott & Company, 1880), 14.

[198] Carl Hovey, *Stonewall Jackson* (Small, Maynard & Company, 1900), 89.

"The time for war has not yet come, but it will come, and that soon; and when it does come, my advice is to draw the sword and throw away the scabbard."[199]

"Who could not conquer with such troops as these?"[200]

"Shoot the brave officers, and the cowards will run away and take the men with them."[201]

"This army stays here until the last wounded man is removed. Before I will leave them to the enemy, I will lose many more men."[202]

"My troops may sometimes fail in driving an enemy from a position; but the enemy fails to drive my men from a position."[203]

"Close up, men, close up; push on, push on."[204]

"Never take counsel of your fears."[205]

"Arms is a profession that, if its principles are adhered to for success, requires an officer do what he fears may be wrong and yet, according to military experience, must be done, if success is to be attained."[206]

---

[199] Donald A. Davis, *Stonewall Jackson* (Palgrave Macmillan, 2007), 42.
[200] William C. Chase, *Story of Stonewall Jackson: A Narrative of the Career of Thomas Jonathan (Stonewall) Jackson, from Written and Verbal Accounts of His Life* (D. E. Luther Publishing Company, 1901), 429.
[201] Steven E. Woodworth, *The Loyal, True, and Brave: America's Civil War Soldiers* (Rowman & Littlefield, 2002), 65.
[202] Mary Anna Jackson, *Life and letters of General Thomas J. Jackson* (Harper & Brothers, 1892), 247.
[203] Frank Moore, *The Portrait Gallery of the War, Civil, Military, and Naval: A Biographical Record* (D. Van Nostrand, 1865), 124.
[204] James I. Robertson, *The Stonewall Brigade* (LSU Press, 1978), 143.
[205] Ethan Sepp Rafuse, *Stonewall Jackson: A Biography* (ABC-CLIO, 2011), 76.
[206] Mary Anna Jackson, *Memoirs of Stonewall Jackson* (Louisville: The Prentice Press, 1895), 249.

"Our God was my shield. His protecting care is an additional cause for gratitude."[207]

"So far as I can see, my course was a wise one; the best that I could do under the circumstances, though very distasteful to my feelings; and I hope and pray to Our Heavenly Father that I may never again be circumstanced as on that day."[208]

"Sacrifices! Have I not made them? What is my life here but a daily sacrifice?"[209]

"If you desire to be more heavenly minded, think more of the things of heaven, and less of the things of earth."[210]

"No, No, you greatly overestimate my capacity for usefulness. A better man will soon be sent to take my place."[211]

"What is life without honor? Degradation is worse than death."[212]

A favorite maxim of Jackson's was, "Duty is ours; consequences are God's."[213]

"If I know myself, all I am and all I have is at the service of my country."[214]

---

[207] Ibid., 247.

[208] Ibid., 249.

[209] William C. Chase, *Story of Stonewall Jackson: A Narrative of the Career of Thomas Jonathan (Stonewall) Jackson, from Written and Verbal Accounts of His Life* (D. E. Luther Publishing Company, 1901), 295.

[210] Mary Anna Jackson, *Life and letters of General Thomas J. Jackson* (Harper & Brothers, 1892), 85.

[211] Ibid., 233.

[212] John Esten Cooke, Moses Drury Hoge, John William Jones, *Stonewall Jackson: A Military Biography* (New York: A. Appleton and Company, 1876), 554.

[213] William C. Chase, *Story of Stonewall Jackson: A Narrative of the Career of Thomas Jonathan (Stonewall) Jackson, from Written and Verbal Accounts of His Life* (D. E. Luther Publishing Company, 1901), 481.

[214] Allen Tate, *Stonewall Jackson: The Good Soldier* (Rowman & Littlefield, 1991), 62.

"People who are anxious to bring on war don't know what they are bargaining for; they don't see all the horrors that must accompany such an event."[215]

"It is painful enough to discover with what unconcern they speak of war and threaten it. I have seen enough of it to make me look upon it as the sum of all evils."[216]

"I am in favor of making a thorough trial for peace, and if we fail in this and our state is invaded, to defend it with terrific resistance."[217]

"So great is my confidence in General Lee that I am willing to follow him blindfolded."[218]

"You may be whatever you resolve to be."[219]

"Don't say it's impossible! Turn your command over to the next officer. If he can't do it, I'll find someone who can, even if I have to take him from the ranks!"[220]

"Never fight against heavy odds, if by any possible maneuvering you can hurl your own force on only a part, and that the weakest part, of your enemy and crush it. Such tactics will win every time, and a small army may thus destroy a large one in detail, and repeated victory will make it invincible."[221]

---

[215] Thomas Jackson Arnold, *Early Life and Letters of General Thomas J. Jackson: "Stonewall" Jackson* (Fleming H. Revell Company, 1916), 294.

[216] G. F. E. Henderson, *Stonewall Jackson and the American Civil War, Volume 1* (New York: Longmans, Green and Company, 1909), 103.

[217] Thomas Jackson Arnold, *Early Life and Letters of General Thomas J. Jackson: "Stonewall" Jackson* (Fleming H. Revell Company, 1916), 294.

[218] Arthur C. Inman, ed., *Soldier of the South: General Pickett's War Letters to Hid Wife* (Boston & New York: Houghton Mifflin Company, 1928), 27-28.

[219] Carl Hovey, *Stonewall Jackson* (Small, Maynard & Company, 1900), 8.

[220] Robert G. Tanner, *Stonewall in the Valley: Thomas J. 'Stonewall' Jackson's Shenandoah Valley Campaign, Spring 1862* (Stackpole Books, 2002), 348.

[221] Elihu Samuel Riley, *Stonewall Jackson: A Thesaurus of Ancedotes of and Incidents in the Life of Lieut. General Jonathan Jackson, C.S.A.* (Elihu Samuel Riley, 1920), 7.

"Why should Christians be disturbed about the dissolution of the Union? It can only come by God's permission, and will only be permitted if for His people's good. I cannot see why we should be distressed about such things, whatever be their consequence."[222]

"It is the Lord's day; my wish is fulfilled. I always wanted to die on Sunday."[223]

"... war is a contest of brains. It is the generals who do the fighting, so to speak, and not the soldiers. If one overcomes the other, and defeats or destroys his army, the inquirer will not have to go very far to discover the reason. One side is victor because the general was a better master of the art of making war than his opponent because his plans were deeper, his insight into those of the enemy more penetrating, his execution more rapid, or his nerve more steady and indomitable."[224]

"If I can deceive my own friends, I can make certain of deceiving the enemy."[225]

"You see me severely wounded, but not depressed—not unhappy. I believe it has been done according to God's holy will, and I acquiesce entirely in it. You may think it strange; but you never saw me more perfectly contented that I am today; for I am sure that my Heavenly Father designs this affliction for my good. I am perfectly satisfied that either in this life, or in that which is to come, I shall discover that what is now regarded as a calamity is a blessing. And if it appears a great calamity (as it surely will be a great inconvenience) to be deprived of my arm, it will result in a great blessing. I can wait until God in his own time shall make known to me the object he has in thus afflicting me. But why should I not rather rejoice in it as a blessing, and not

---

[222] G. F. E. Henderson, *Stonewall Jackson and the American Civil War, Volume 1* (New York: Longmans, Green and Company, 1909), 211.
[223] John Esten Cooke, Moses Drury Hoge, John William Jones, *Stonewall Jackson: A Military Biography* (New York: A. Appleton and Company, 1876), 484.
[224] Stonewall Jackson, *The life of Stonewall Jackson: From Official Papers, Contemporary Narratives, and Personal Acquaintance* (Richardson, 1863), 272.
[225] John Selby, *Stonewall Jackson as Military Commander* (Barnes & Noble Publishing, 1968), 72.

look on it as a calamity at all? If it were in my power to replace my arm, I would not dare to do it unless I could know that it was the will of my heavenly Father."[226]

"My comfort has nothing in the world to do with it, sir. You, as my pastor, you think that it is my duty to lead in public prayer—I think so too—and by God's help I mean to do it. I wish that you would call on me more frequently."[227]

General Jackson's last order given: "The danger is all over. The enemy is routed! Go back and tell A. P. Hill to press forward!"[228]

"If the enemy does come, I am not afraid of them. I have always been kind to their wounded, and I am sure they will be kind to me."[229]

"It has been a precious experience to me that I was brought face to face with death and found that all was well."[230]

Major General James Ewell Brown Stuart

"During the afternoon, he asked Dr. Brewer whether it were not possible for him to survive the night. The doctor frankly told him that death was close at hand. "He then said: 'I am resigned if it be God's will; but I would like to see my wife. But God's will be done.' "Again he said to Dr. Brewer: 'I am

---

[226] John Esten Cooke, Moses Drury Hoge, John William Jones, *Stonewall Jackson: A Military Biography* (New York: A. Appleton and Company, 1876), 505.

[227] *The Chautauquan, Volume 30* (Chautauqua Press, 1900), 85.

[228] Elihu Samuel Riley, *Stonewall Jackson: A Thesaurus of Ancedotes of and Incidents in the Life of Lieut. General Jonathan Jackson, C.S.A.* (Elihu Samuel Riley, 1920), 193.

[229] William C. Chase, *Story of Stonewall Jackson: A Narrative of the Career of Thomas Jonathan (Stonewall) Jackson, from Written and Verbal Accounts of His Life* (D. E. Luther Publishing Company, 1901), 481.

[230] Mary Anna Jackson, *Memoirs of Stonewall Jackson* (Louisville: The Prentice Press, 1895), 442.

going fast now; I am resigned. God's will be done.'"[231]

"Believe you can whip the enemy and you have won half the battle."[232]

"Believing that the hand of God was clearly manifested in the deliverance of my command from danger and the crowning success attending it, I ascribe to him the praise, the honor, and the glory."[233]

JEB Stuart received the news of his daughter's (Flora) death: "If my darling's case is hopeless, there are ten chances to one that I will get to Lynchburg too late; if she is convalescent, why should my presence be necessary? She was sick nine days before I knew it. Let us trust in the good God who has blessed us so much, that He will spare our child to us, but if it should please Him to take her from us, let us bear it with Christian fortitude and resignation."[234]

"Remember that we gallop toward the enemy, and trot away, always."[235]

"I would rather be a private in Virginia's army than a general in any army that was going to coerce her."[236]

"Then all advanced in as perfect order as if they had been on parade, their bayonets sparkling in the light of the setting sun and their red battle flags dancing gayly in the breeze."[237]

---

[231] Mary L. Williamson, *The life of J. E. B. Stuart* (Richmond: B.F. Johnson & Company, 1914), 188.

[232] George Walsh, *Damage Them All You Can: Robert E. Lee's Army of Northern Virginia* (Macmillan, 2003), 308.

[233] Mary L. Williamson, *The life of J. E. B. Stuart* (Richmond: B.F. Johnson & Company, 1914), 106.

[234] Ibid., 112.

[235] Emory M. Thomas, *Bold Dragon: The Life of JEB Stuart* (University of Oklahoma Press, 1999), 72.

[236] H. W. Crocker, *The Politically Incorrect Guide to the Civil War* (Regnery Publishing, 2008), 310.

[237] W. W. Blackford, *War Years With JEB Stuart* (New York: Charles Scribner's Sons, 1946), 121.

"Well, I don't know how this will turn out, but if it is God's will that I shall die, I am ready."[238]

"In all these operations I deem it my duty to bear testimony to the gallant and patient endurance of the cavalry, fighting every day most unequal conflicts, and successfully opposing for an extraordinary period the onward march of McClellan."[239]

"In case of an advance of the enemy, you will offer such resistance as will be justifiable to check him and discover his intentions; and, if possible, you will prevent him from gaining possession of the gaps."[240]

"Blessed be God that giveth us victory."[241]

"May God give us the victory and cover our heads in the day of battle."[242]

"Believing that the hand of God was clearly manifest in the signal deliverance of my command from danger and the crowning success attending to it, I ascribe to Him the praise, the honor, and the glory."[243]

"All I asked is that I may be killed leading a cavalry charge."[244]

---

[238] Lena Young De Grumond Delaune, *JEB Stuart* (Pelican Publishing, 1962), 154.

[239] H. B. McClelland, *The Life and Campaigns of Major-General J.E.B. Stuart, Commander of the Cavalry of the Army of Northern Virginia* (New York: Houghton, Mifflin & Company, 1885), 185.

[240] John S. Mosby, *Mosby's War Reminiscences and Stuart's Cavalry Campaigns* (Boston: George A. Jones & Company, Publishers, 1887), 204.

[241] John William Thomason, *JEB Stuart* (University of Nebraska Press, 1994), 136.

[242] Ibid., 10.

[243] Douglas Southall Freeman, *Lee's Lieutenants: Cedar Mountain to Chancellorsville* (Simon and Schuster, 1997), 303.

[244] Cormac O'Brien, *Secret Lives of the Civil War: What Your Teachers Never Told You about the War Between the States* (Quirk Books, 2007), 266.

"Go back, go back and do your duty as I have done mine, and our country will be safe. Go back! Go back! I had rather die than be whipped."[245]

"I realize that if we oppose force to force we cannot win, for their resources are greater than ours. We must make up in quality what we lack in numbers. We must substitute esprit for numbers. Therefore, I strive to inculcate in my men the spirit of the chase...."[246]

"I rejoice to that I still have evidence of a Savior's pardoning love ... and prayed God to guide me in the right way and teach me to walk as a Christian should. When I came here I had reason to expect that many and strong temptations would beset my path, but I relied on 'him whom to know is live [life] everlasting' to deliver me from temptation, and prayed God to guide me in the right way and teach way to walk as a Christian should; I have never for a moment hesitated to persevere...."[247]

"Ours is a glorious country. I love it but like Mr. [John C.] Calhoun, while I love the Union I love Virginia more and if one attachment ever becomes incompatible with the other I scruple not to say 'Virginia shall command my poor services.'"[248]

"For my part, I have no hesitancy from the first that, right or wrong, alone or otherwise, I go with Virginia."[249]

"I have a reputation of being fond of saying, 'no' but I have had but one rule of action from the first and that was duty."[250]

---

[245] Henry Brainerd McClellan, *The Life and Campaigns of Major-General J. E. B. Stuart, Commander of the Cavalry of the Army of Northern Virginia* (Houghton, Mifflin, 1885), 415.

[246] John William Thomason, *JEB Stuart* (University of Nebraska Press, 1994), 9.

[247] Emory M. Thomas, *Bold Dragoon: The Life of J.E.B. Stuart* (University of Oklahoma Press, 1999), 14.

[248] Jeffry D. Wert, *Cavalryman of the Lost Cause: A Biography of J. E. B. Stuart* (New York: Simon and Schuster, 2008), 36.

[249] Ibid., 43.

[250] John William Thomason, *JEB Stuart* (University of Nebraska Press, 1994), 11.

"You need not be surprised to see your hubbie a Brigadier. I have been in one real battle now & feel sure that I can command better than many I saw."[251]

"You know, I make duty paramount to everything."[252]

"A military man without aspirations is like a vessel without sail — a compass without the needle."[253]

"I never expect to come out of this war alive."[254]

"You're mistaken, Freed, I don't love bullets any better than you do. It is my duty to go where they are sometimes, but I don't expect to survive the war."[255]

"Go ahead old fellow: I know you will do what is right."[256]

"I wish an assurance on your part in the other event your surviving me, that you will make the land for which I have given my life your home, and keep my offspring on Southern soil."[257]

"You will find in my hat a small Confederate flag, which a lady of Columbia, South Carolina, sent me, with the request that I would wear it upon my horse in a battle and return it to her."[258]

---

[251] Arnold M. Pavlovsky, *Riding in Circles: J.E.B. Stuart and the Confederate Cavalry 1861-1862* (Arnold M. Pavlovsky, 2010), 254.

[252] Jeffry D. Wert, *Cavalryman of the Lost Cause: A Biography of J. E. B. Stuart* (New York: Simon and Schuster, 2009), 237.

[253] Arnold M. Pavlovsky, *Riding in Circles: J.E.B. Stuart and the Confederate Cavalry 1861-1862* (Arnold M. Pavlovsky, 2010), 247.

[254] Jeffry D. Wert, *Cavalryman of the Lost Cause: A Biography of J. E. B. Stuart* (New York: Simon and Schuster, 2009), 337.

[255] Robert J. Trout, *They Followed the Plume: The Story of J.E.B. Stuart and His Staff* (Stackpole Books, 2003), 288-289.

[256] John William Thomason, *JEB Stuart* (University of Nebraska Press, 1994), 499.

[257] Jeffry D. Wert, *Cavalryman of the Lost Cause: A Biography of J. E. B. Stuart* (New York: Simon and Schuster, 2009), 367.

[258] Henry B. McClellan, *I Rode With JED Stuart: The Life and Campaigns of Major General JEB Stuart* (Da Capo Press, 1994), 416.

"My spurs which I have always worn in battle I promised to give to Mrs. Lilly Lee of Shepherdstown, Virginia. My sword I leave to my son."[259]

"In times like these, when Patriots stand aghast at the threatened overthrow of a government that for nearly one hundred years has been the theme of admiration with statesmen and philosophers that has defied alike the frowns of despotism on the one hand, and the storms of anarchy on the other...."[260]

"General Lee, their right rests on the Brock road, and the Brock road is as clean of defences as if gunpowder had never been invented, nor breastworks thought of!"[261]

"We seized and brought over a large number of horses, the property of citizens of the United States. The valuable information obtained in this reconnaissance, as to the distribution of the enemy's force, was communicated orally to the Commanding General, and need not be here repeated. A number of public functionaries and prominent citizens were taken captive and brought over as hostages for our own unoffending citizens, whom the enemy had torn from their homes, and confined in dungeons in the North. The results of this expedition, in a moral and political point of view, can hardly be estimated, and the consternation among property-holders in Pennsylvania was beyond description. Believing that the hand of God was clearly manifested in the signal deliverance of my command from danger, and the crowning success attending it, I ascribe to Him the praise, the honour, and the glory."[262]

---

[259] Ibid., 416.

[260] Arnold M. Pavlovsky, *Riding in Circles: J.E.B. Stuart and the Confederate Cavalry 1861-1862* (Arnold M. Pavlovsky, 2010), 164-165.

[261] Mary Johnston, *The Long Role* (Toronto: Houghton Mifflin Company, 1911), 660.

[262] Edward A. Pollard, *Lee and His Lieutenants: Comparing the Early Life, Public Services, and Campaigns of General Robert E. Lee and His Companion In Arms, With a Record of the Campaigns and Heroic Deeds* (New York: E. B. Treat and Company, 1867), 429.

"Tell Gen. Lee that all is right. Jackson has not advanced, but I have; and I am going to crowd them with artillery."[263]

"I would give anything to make a pilgrimage to the old place and when the war is over to quietly spend the rest of my days there."[264]

"You might have shot a marble at them — but I am not afraid of any ball aimed at me."[265]

"The horseman who, at his officer's bidding, without question, leaps into unexplored darkness, knowing nothing except that there is danger ahead, possesses the highest attribute of the patriot soldier. It is a great source of pride to me to command a division of such men."[266]

"I beg to urge that in no case should persons not connected with the army, and who are amply compensated for all that is taken, be allowed more subsistence per day than the noble veterans who are periling their lives in the cause and at every sacrifice are enduring hardship and exposure in the ranks."[267]

"I have the honor to report that 'circumstances' were such that they could have seen me if they had stopped to look behind, and I answered both at the cannon's mouth. Judging from his speed, Griffin surely left for Washington to hurry up that dinner."[268]

---

[263] Mary Johnston, *The Long Role* (Toronto: Houghton Mifflin Company, 1911), 429.

[264] Henry Brainerd McClellan, *The Life and Campaigns of Major-General J. E. B. Stuart, Commander of the Cavalry of the Army of Northern Virginia* (Houghton, Mifflin, 1885), 6.

[265] Gamaliel Bradford, *Confederate Portraits* (Houghton Mifflin Company, 1914), 37.

[266] Ibid., 39.

[267] Ibid., 40.

[268] Ibid., 54.

Major General Albert Sidney Johnston

"To continue to hold my commission after being apprised of the final action of my State, to whose partiality in a great measure I owe my position, could find no justification in my own conscience; and I have, therefore, this day forwarded the resignation of my commission for the acceptance of the President, which I hope may be promptly accepted. I have asked that my successor be appointed and ordered to relieve me as soon as practicable." [269]

"I felt, as soon as I learned the course adopted by my State (Texas), that it was my duty to conform to her will, and that I ought to forward my resignation to the President ; and I have accordingly done so. I have served faithfully to the present moment, and will continue to until I am properly relieved. Until then, rest assured that I will do nothing inconsistent with my obligations to the Government as an officer. The pressure of Northern views had begun to manifest itself in the army, and therefore I felt less repugnance in severing my connection with it. You will allow that a man's convictions of the necessity must be strong to lead him to take the step I have done. I have counseled only with my wife." [270]

"You will, in order to cover the northern line occupied by the Confederate army in this department, and threatened by the army of the United States, concentrate your command at Bowling Green, Kentucky, and secure and hold this important point in our line of defense.... Secrecy in preparation and promptness in execution give the best, if not the only, promise of success; and the general is confident you will be wanting in neither." [271]

"It is more likely to be a seven years' war." [272]

---

[269] William Preston Johnston, *The Life of Gen. Albert Sidney Johnston, Embracing His Services in the Armies of the United States, The Republic of Texas, and the Confederate States* (New York: D. Appleton Company, 1878), 271.
[270] Ibid., 272.
[271] Ibid., 310.
[272] Ibid., 333.

"I will use all means to increase my force, and spare no exertion to render it effective, at any point; but I cannot assure you that this will be sufficient, and, if reinforcements from less endangered or less important points can be spared, I would be glad to receive them."[273]

"I am disappointed in the state of public sentiment in the South. Our people seem to have suffered from a violent political fever, which has left them exhausted. They are not up to the revolutionary point, I replied, "The logic of your remark, general, is that you doubt our success? "He looked at me gravely for a moment, and said, 'If the South wishes to be free, she can be free.'"[274]

"I prefer volunteers for the war, as securing better disciplined, more skilled, and more effective forces. But dispatch, now, is of the first importance; and, therefore, companies, battalions, and regiments, offering for twelve months will be at once received."[275]

"I would fight them if they were a million."[276]

"We may be annihilated, but we cannot be conquered."[277]

Major General Patrick Ronayne Cleburne

"I am with the South in life or in death, in victory or defeat. I never owned a negro and care nothing for them, but these people have been my friends and have stood up to me on all occasions. In addition to this, I believe the North is about to wage a brutal and unholy war on a people who have done them no wrong, in violation of the Constitution and the fundamental principles of the government.... We propose no invasion of the North, no attack on them, and only ask to be let alone."[278]

---

[273] Ibid., 338.
[274] Ibid., 340.
[275] Ibid., 340.
[276] Grady McWhiney, Perry D. Jamieson, *Attack and Die: Civil War Military Tactics and the Southern Heritage* (University of Alabama Press, 1984), 162.
[277] Iain C. Martin, *The Quotable American Civil War* (Lyons Press, 2008), 66.
[278] Glenn Dedmondt, *The Flags of Civil War Arkansas* (Pelican Publishing, 2009), 78.

"Every man should endeavor to understand the meaning of subjugation before it is too late.... It means the history of this heroic struggle will be written by the enemy; that our youth will be trained by Northern schoolteachers; will learn from Northern school books their version of the war; will be impressed by the influences of history and education to regard our gallant dead as traitors, and our maimed veterans as fit objects for derision... It is said slavery is all we are fighting for, and if we give it up we give up all. Even if this were true, which we deny, slavery is not all our enemies are fighting for. It is merely the pretense to establish sectional superiority and a more centralized form of government, and to deprive us of our rights and liberties."[279]

"Surrender means that the history of this heroic struggle will be written by the enemy; that the youth will be trained by Northern school teachers; will learn from Northern school books their version of the War; will be impressed by all the influences of history and education to regard our gallant dead as traitors, and our maimed veterans as fit subjects for derision."[280]

"If all in the South fought like the Irish, Secession would long since be an accomplished fact."[281]

"Friend and foe learned to watch for the blue flag that marked where Cleburne was in battle. Where his division defended no odds broke its lines, where it attack, no numbers resisted its onslaught, save only once, and there's the grave of Cleburne and his heroic division."[282]

"If this cause, that is dear to my heart, is doomed to fail, I pray Heaven may let me fail with it, while my face is toward the enemy and my arm battling for that which I know is right."[283]

---

[279] Howell Purdue, Elizabeth Purdue, *Pat Cleburne, Confederate General: A Definitive Biography* (Hill Jr. College Press, 1973), 454.

[280] Irving A. Buck, *Cleburne and His Command* (New York, The Neale Publishing Company, 1908), 215-222.

[281] John Francis McGuire, *The Irish In America* (New York: D & J Saldier & Company, 1880), 572.

[282] Howell Purdue, Elizabeth Purdue, Pat Cleburne, *Confederate General: A Definitive Biography* (Hill Jr. College Press, 1973), 189.

[283] Ibid., 388.

Lieutenant General John Bell Hood

"I knew that if the feat was accomplished it must be at a most fearful sacrifice of as brave and gallant soldiers as ever engaged in battle."[284]

"After this urgent protest against entering into battle at Gettysburg according to instructions - which protest is the first and only one I ever made during my entire military career — I ordered my line to advance and make the assault."[285]

"As to their gallantry and unflinching courage, they stand unsurpassed in the history of the world."[286]

"Soldiers—I had hoped that when we left our winter-quarters, it would be to move forward; but those who have better opportunities of judging than we have, order otherwise. You must not regard it as a disgrace—it is never a disgrace to retreat when the welfare of your country requires such a movement. Ours is the last Brigade to leave the lines of the Potomac. Upon us devolves the duties of a rear guard, and in order to discharge them faithfully, every man must be in his place, at all-times. You are now leaving your comfortable winter-quarters to enter upon a stirring campaign—a campaign which will be filled with blood, and fraught with the destinies of our young Confederacy. Its success or failure rests upon the soldiers of the South. They are equal to the emergency. I feel no hesitation in predicting that you, at least, will discharge your duties, and when the struggle does come, that proud banner you bear, placed by the hand of beauty in the keeping of the brave, will ever be found in the thickest of the fray.—Fellow-soldiers—Texans—let us stand or fall together. I have done."[287]

---

[284] John B. Hood, *Advance and Retreat, Personal Experiences in the United States and Confederate States Armies* (New Orleans: Hood Orphan Memorial Fund, 1880), 58.

[285] Ibid., 59.

[286] C. M. Winkler, *The Life and Character of General John B. Hood* (Austin, Texas: Droughon & Lambert, Printer, 1885), 18.

[287] Nicholas A Davis, *The Campaign From Texas to Maryland With the Battle of Fredericksburg* (Richmond: Presbyterian Committee of Publication of the Confederate States, 1863), 24-25.

Forward, forward, charge right down on them, and drive them out with the bayonet."[288]

"… *directing in person the 4th Texas, they were the first to pierce the strong line of breast-works occupied by the enemy, which caused great confusion in their ranks. And here the 18th Georgia, commanded by Colonel Ruff, came to the support of the 4th, pressed over the hotly contested field, inclining from right to left, with the 5th Texas on their left, taking a large number of prisoners, and fourteen pieces of artillery. The guns were taken by the 4th Texas and 18th Georgia, and the prisoners by the 5th Texas."*[289]

"*Here I witnessed the most terrible clash of arms by far that has occurred during the war. The two little giant brigades of my command wrestled with the mighty force, and although they lost hundreds of their officers and men, they drove them from their position, and forced them to abandon their guns on our left. One of these brigades numbered only eight hundred and fifty-four (854) men."*[290]

General Hood remarked, that he was "*thoroughly of the opinion, that the victory of that day, would have been as thorough, quick and complete, as on the Plains of Manassas, on the 30th of August, if General McClaws had reached the field with his men, even as late as 9 o'clock."*[291]

"*After this urgent protest against entering the battle at Gettysburg, according to instructions—which protest is the first and only one I ever made during my entire military career—I ordered my line to advance and make the assault."*[292]

---

[288] Ibid., 55.

[289] Ibid., 58.

[290] John B. Hood, *Advance and Retreat, Personal Experiences in the United States and Confederate States Armies* (New Orleans: Hood Orphan Memorial Fund, 1880), 45.

[291] Nicholas A Davis, *The Campaign From Texas to Maryland With the Battle of Fredericksburg* (Richmond: Presbyterian Committee of Publication of the Confederate States, 1863), 92.

[292] John B. Hood, *Advance and Retreat, Personal Experiences in the United States and Confederate States Armies* (New Orleans: Hood Orphan Memorial Fund, 1880), 59.

"This affair, which brought the brigade so suddenly and unexpectedly under fire for the first time, sensed as a happy introduction to the enemy."[293]

"Whilst I acknowledge with pleasure the gallant conduct and efficient service of the Georgia State troops in the defence of Atlanta, I cannot conceive how they could have been expected to accomplish all that General Johnston seems to have anticipated...."[294]

"Advance and Retreat:" *"I do this day and hour, in the name of truth, honor and justice, in the name of the departed soul of the Christian and noble Polk, and in the presence of the Creator, most solemnly deny that General Polk or I recommended General Johnston, at Carsville, to retreat when he intended to give battle; and affirm that the recommendation made by us to change his position was throughout the discussion coupled with the proviso, if he did not intend to force a pitched battle with General Sheriman."*[295]

"Moreover, the highest perfection in the education of troops well disciplined can only be attained through continued appeals to their pride and through incitement to make known their prowess by the substantial test of guns and colors captured upon the field of battle. Soldiers thus educated will ever prove a terror to the foe."[296]

"Soldiers—In obedience to orders from the War Department I assume command of this army and department. I feel the weight of the responsibility so suddenly and unexpectedly devolved upon me by this position, and shall bend all my energies and employ all my skill to meet its requirements. I look with confidence to your patriotism to stand by me, and rely upon your prowess to wrest your country from the grasp of the invader, entitling yourselves to the proud distinction of being called the deliverers of an oppressed people."[297]

---

[293] J. B. Polley, *Hoods Texas Brigade: It's Marches, It's Battles, It's Achievements* (New York: The Neale Publishing Company, 1910), 24.

[294] John B. Hood, *Advance and Retreat, Personal Experiences in the United States and Confederate States Armies* (New Orleans: Hood Orphan Memorial Fund, 1880), 146.

[295] C. M. Winkler, *The Life and Character of Gen. John B. Hood* (Austin: Draughton & Lambert Printers, 1885), 27.

[296] Ibid., 29.

[297] William P. Snow, *Lee and His Generals* (New York: The Fairfax Press,

"Soldiers, it is not my province to make speeches: I was not born for such work; that I leave to other men. Within a few days I expect to give the command 'forward,' and I believe you are, like myself, willing to go forward, even if we live on parched corn and beef. I am ready to give the command 'forward' this very night. Good-night."[298]

"Headquarters, Army of Tennessee, near Nashville,
Dec. 8, via Mobile, Dec. 9, 1864.
To Hon. J. A. Seddon:

About four o'clock p. m., November 30th, we attacked the enemy at Franklin, and drove them from their centre line of temporary works into the inner lines, which they evacuated during the night, leaving their dead and wounded in our possession, and retired to Nashville, closely followed by our cavalry. We captured several stands of colors and about one thousand prisoners. Our troops fought with great gallantry. We have to lament the loss of many gallant officers and men. Major-general Cleburne and Brigadier-generals John Williams, Adams, Gist, Strahl, and Granberry were killed. Major-general John Brown, and Brigadier-generals S. Carter, Manigault, Quarles, Cockerill, and Scott were wounded. Brigadier-general Gordon was captured."[299]

"Our loss of officers was excessively large in proportion to the loss of men."[300]

"Headquarters, Army op the Tennessee,
Tupelo, Miss., Jan. 23, 1865.

Soldiers—At my request, I have this day been relieved from the command of the army. In taking leave of you, accept my thanks for the patience with which you have endured your hardships during the recent campaign. I am alone responsible for its conception, and strove hard to do my duty in its execution. I urge upon you the importance of giving your entire support to the distinguished soldier who now assumes command, and shall look with deep interest on all your future operations, and rejoice at your success."[301]

1982), 409-410.
[298] William Parker Snow, *Southern General: Their Live and Campaigns* (New York: Charles B. Richardson, 1866), 414.
[299] Ibid., 416.
[300] Ibid., 416.
[301] Ibid., 417.

"... while I myself do not know where we are going, I can assure you that such of you as keep up with your command, will witness and take part in stirring and glorious events."[302]

"'General Hood, where is the splendid division you had this morning?' Hood replied, 'They are lying on the field where you sent them, sir; but few have straggled. My division has been almost wiped out.'"[303]

"Detail an officer and twenty-five of your best men, Colonel, and have them report to me at my headquarters within an hour. I have set my heart on securing possession of one of those gunboats down on the Nansemond River, and I feel sure that many men can easily capture it."[304]

"General Hood said of his me: 'As to their gallantry and unflinching courage, they stand unsurpassed in the history of the world.'"[305]

Lieutenant General Wade Hampton

"I want you to try to teach to your children and to your children's children that ours was not a lost cause. I want you to tell them that we were fighting for the right ..."[306]

"If we were wrong in the contest, then the Declaration of Independence of 1776 was a grave mistake and the revolution to which it led was a crime... If Washington was a patriot, Lee cannot have been a rebel; if the enunciation of the grand truths in the Declaration of Independence made Jefferson immortal, the observance of them could not have made Davis a traitor."[307]

---

[302] J. B. Polley, *Hoods Texas Brigade: It's Marches, It's Battles, It's Achievements* (New York: The Neale Publishing Company, 1910), 35.
[303] Ibid., 134.
[304] Ibid., 143.
[305] C. M. Winkler, *The Life and Character of General John B. Hood* (Austin, Texas: Droughon & Lambert, Printer, 1885), 18.
[306] Walter Brian Cisco, Wade Hampton, *Confederate Warrior, Conservative Statesman* (Potomac Books, 2004), 323.
[307] Ibid., 319.

"Watch me, boys; do as I do."[308]

"During this time a period of twenty-three days the command had no rest, was badly supplied with rations and forage marched upwards of 400 miles fought the greater portion of six days and one entire night captured upwards of 2,000 prisoners, many guns, small arms, wagons, horses, and other material of war, and was completely successful in defeating two of the most formidable and well-organized expeditions of the enemy. This was accomplished at a cost, in my division, of 719 killed, wounded and missing. The men have borne their privations with perfect cheerfulness; they have fought admirably, and I wish to express, before closing my reports, not only my thanks to them for their good conduct, but my pride at having had the honour to command them."[309]

He said this of General Sherman: "Your line of march can be traced by the lurid light of burning houses; and in more than one household there is an agony far more bitter than death a crime too black to be mentioned."[310]

Lieutenant General Nathan Bedford Forrest

"Comrades, through the years of bloodshed and many marches you were tried and true soldiers. So through years of peace you have been good citizens, and now that we are again united under the old flag, I love it as I did in the days of my youth, and I feel sure that you love it also."[311]

"There is no doubt we could soon wipe old Sherman off the face of the earth,

---

[308] William P. Snow, *Lee and His Generals* (New York: Richardson and Company, 1867), 494.

[309] Edward A. Pollard, *Lee and His Lieutenants: Comparing the Early Life, Public Services, and Campaigns of General Robert E. Lee and His Companion In Arms, With a Record of the Campaigns and Heroic Deeds* (New York: E. B. Treat and Company, 1867), 743.

[310] Ibid., 744.

[311] John Allan Wyeth, *Life of General Nathan Bedford Forrest* (New York: Harper & Brothers, 1899), 620.

John, if they'd give me enough men and you enough guns."[312]

"Preserve untarnished the reputation you have so nobly won."[313]

"When asked in later years how he explained the success achieved in his many battles, he replied: 'I do not know, unless it was because I generally got there first with the most men.'"[314]

"I loved the old government in 1861; I loved the old Constitution yet. I think it is the best government in the world, if administered as it was before the war. I do not hate it; I am opposing now only the radical revolutionists who are trying to destroy it. I believe that party to be composed, as I know it is in Tennessee, of the worst men on Gods earth — men who would hesitate at no crime, and who have only one object in view — to enrich themselves."[315]

"Never stand and take a charge ... charge them too."[316]

"After the war Forrest would boast, 'I was one horse ahead at the end.'"[317]

"War means fighting, and fighting means killing."[318]

"I have never on the field of battle sent you where I was unwilling to go myself, nor would I now advise you to go a course which I myself unwilling

---

[312] John Watson Morton, *The Artillery of Nathan Bedford Forrest's Cavalry: The Wizard of the Saddle* (Publishing house of the M. E. Church, South, Smith & Lamar, agents, 1909), 258.

[313] John Allan Wyeth, *Life of Lieutenant-General Nathan Bedford Forrest* (New York: Harper & Brothers Publishers, 1908), 611.

[314] Ibid., 33.

[315] Jack Hurst, *Nathan Bedford Forrest: A Biography* (Random House LLC, 1994), 313.

[316] John Allan Wyeth, *Life of Lieutenant-General Nathan Bedford Forrest* (New York: Harper & Brothers Publishers, 1908), 160.

[317] William J. Bennett, *America: The Last Best Hope Volumes I and II* (Thomas Nelson Inc, 2007), 361.

[318] John Watson Morton, *The Artillery of Nathan Bedford Forrest's Cavalry: The Wizard of the Saddle* (Publishing house of the M. E. Church, South, Smith & Lamar, agents, 1909), 307.

to pursue. You have been good soldiers, you can be good citizens. Obey the laws, preserve your honor, and to the Government to which you have surrendered can afford to be and will be magnanimous."[319]

"It is believed that the expedition has done great good in giving countenance to the Southern sympathizers in this region, and of disabusing the minds of the Union people, who expected every species of outrage at the hands of the Confederate soldiers. Not a few assured us that they would no longer use their influence against the cause of the South. Universal kindness was the part of the officers in command."[320]

"No one could do justice in description to the attack or the defence. More determination could not have been exhibited by the attacking party, while more coolness and bravery never were manifested than were seen in our artillerists. Never were men more jubilant than when victory crowned the steady bravery of our little force."[321]

"I returned to my quarters, and sent out two men, who, going by the road up the bank of the river, returned without seeing any of the enemy only fires, which I believe to be the old camp-fires, and so stated to the general; the wind, being very high, had fanned them into a blaze."[322]

"The fight ended about 2.30 P.M., without any change in our relative positions. We were employed the remainder of the evening in gathering up the arms and assisting in getting off the wounded. I was three times over the battle-field, and, late in the evening, was two miles up the river, on the road to the forge. There were none of the enemy in sight when dark came on. Saturday night our troops slept, flushed with victory and confident they could drive the enemy back to the Tennessee River the next morning."[323]

---

[319] John Allan Wyeth, *Life of Lieutenant-General Nathan Bedford Forrest* (New York: Harper & Brothers Publishers, 1908), 614.
[320] John Allan Wyeth, *Life of Lieutenant-General Nathan Bedford Forrest* (New York: Harper & Brothers Publishers, 1908), 29.
[321] Ibid., 47.
[322] *Harper's New Monthly Magazine, Volume 98, Dec 1898-May 1889* (New York: Harper & Brothers, Publishers, 1899), 354.
[323] John Allan Wyeth, *Life of Lieutenant-General Nathan Bedford Forrest* (New York: Harper & Brothers Publishers, 1908), 66-67.

"COLONEL, I must demand an unconditional surrender of your force as prisoners of war, or I will have every man put to the sword. You are aware of the overpowering force I have at my command, and this demand is made to prevent the effusion of blood. I am, Colonel, very respectfully, your obedient servant, N. B. FORREST, To Colonel Lester. Brigadier General of Cavalry, C. S. A."[324]

"In the official report Forrest says: 'Russell's regiment, the Fourth Alabama, charged on horseback, and the enemy became panic-stricken and retreated hastily across Spring Creek, burning the bridge after them. We have heard nothing from them since in that direction.'"[325]

"At this time we occupied the battle-field, and were in possession of the enemy's dead and wounded and three pieces of artillery, and had demanded a surrender. Thirty minutes more would have given us the day, when, to my surprise and astonishment, a fire was opened on us in our rear, and the enemy in heavy force under General J. C. Sullivan advanced on us. Knowing that I had four companies at Clarksburg, on the Huntingdon road, I could not believe that they were Federals until I rode up myself into their lines. The heavy fire of their artillery, unexpected and unlocked for by all, caused a stampede of horses belonging to my dismounted men, who were following up and driving the enemy before them. Finding my men now exposed to fire from both front and rear, I was compelled to withdraw, which I did in good order, leaving behind our dead and wounded. We were able to bring off six pieces of artillery and two caissons. The balance, with the three guns we had captured, we were compelled to leave, as most of the horses were killed or crippled, which rendered it impossible to get them out under the heavy fire of the enemy from both front and rear. Our loss in artillery was three guns and eight caissons, and one piece which burst during the action. We brought off eighty-three prisoners."[326]

---

[324] Jack Hurst, *Nathan Bedford Forrest: A Biography* (Random House LLC, 1994), 101.
[325] John Allan Wyeth, *That Devil Forrest: Life of General Nathan Bedford Forrest* (LSU Press, 1989), 101.
[326] Ibid., 128-129.

"I have no fault to find with my men. In both charges they did their duty as they have always done."[327]

"I am going to have my forces thoroughly organized before I go into the field again. I have ordered dress-parade twice per week."[328]

"By the time the disposition of our force was made, the firing began from the enemy s artillery, and, finding I had no position bearing upon the enemy with my artillery, I ordered Captain S. L. Free man forward with his battery to a high hill, which placed it advantageously for operating on the enemy s left flank. As this was fully half a mile in advance of my first position, I ordered up all the regiments of my brigade on foot to a line parallel with that hill, and nearly at right angles to the pike. I found two regiments of infantry and a regiment of the Federal cavalry posted behind a stone fence to the left of their artillery. A few shells from my guns drove them from their position to the. Light of their battery, and, after about twenty rounds, drove it from its position, retreating by the pike towards Franklin. At this time I was ordered to move forward, and, if possible, get in the rear of the enemy. Ordering up all my troops, we attacked vigorously, and disposed of that portion of the enemy s force moving on the turnpike. The main force of the enemy was posted on the hill in front of Thompson s station and to the left of the pike, and had driven back several times the forces under Generals Arm strong and Whitfield and my two regiments under Colonels Starnes and Edmondson. I now moved Cox s and Biffle's regiments rapidly across the pike in the rear of the enemy, and found they had taken a strong position and were ready to receive us. I immediately ordered the charge, which was led by Biffle and Trezevant, commanding Cox s regiment. The enemy opened a heavy fire upon us, the first volley mortally wounding Lieutenant-Colonel Trezevant and Captain Montgomery Little, who commanded my escort. The men continued to charge to within twenty feet of the Federal line of battle, when the enemy threw down their arms and surrendered."[329]

---

[327] Brian Steel Wills, *A Battle From the Start: The life of Nathan Bedford Forrest* (HarperPerennial, 1993), 102.
[328] John Allan Wyeth, *Life of Lieutenant-General Nathan Bedford Forrest* (New York: Harper & Brothers Publishers, 1908), 154.
[329] Ibid., 163.

"Major, take in a flag of truce, and tell them I have them completely surrounded, and if they don t surrender I ll blow hell out of them in five minutes and won t take one of them alive if I have to sacrifice my men in storming their stockade."[330]

"They succeeded in getting possession of several of the wagons captured at the stockade, and cut out and stampeded the mules. The enemy were repulsed and driven back to Brentwood, but, having no teams, several of the wagons were burned. We brought away three ambulances and harness, nine six-horse wagons and teams and harness, two twohorse wagons, sixty mules and six horses, which were placed in charge of the assistant quartermaster at Columbia. Many of the command who had inferior guns, muskets, shotguns, etc., exchanged them on the field, placing their old guns in the wagons in lieu of them."[331]

"General Van Dorn and I have enough to do fighting the enemies of our country without fighting each other."[332]

"Shoot at everything blue, and keep up the scare."[333]

"Ladies, do not be alarmed, I am General Forrest; I and my men will protect you from harm."[334]

"Immediate surrender your men to be treated as prisoners of war; the officers to retain their side-arms and personal property."[335]

"They advanced in gallant style, driving the enemy back and capturing a battery of artillery, my dismount ed cavalry advancing with them."[336]

---

[330] Ibid., 170.
[331] Ibid., 174.
[332] Robert George Hartje, *Van Dorn: The Life and Times of a Confederate General* (Vanderbilt University Press, 1967), 304.
[333] John Allan Wyeth, *Life of Lieutenant-General Nathan Bedford Forrest* (New York: Harper & Brothers Publishers, 1908), 198.
[334] Ibid., 210.
[335] Ibid., 218.
[336] Ibid., 248.

"Tell General Ector that he need not bother about his right flank, I'll take care of it."[337]

"Is that all you know? Then I'll go there and find out for myself."[338]

"Doctor, if you are alarmed, you may get out of the way; I am as safe here as there."[339]

"Many of my men were broken down and exhausted with climbing the hills on foot and fighting almost constantly for the last nine miles. I determined, therefore, to rely upon the bravery and courage of the few men I had, and advance to the attack. As we moved up, the whole force charged down at a gallop, and I am proud to say that my men did not disappoint me."[340]

"General Grierson left a weak place in his line, and I carried my men right through it."[341]

"If you surrender you shall be treated as prisoners of war, but if I have to storm your works you may expect no quarter."[342]

"I drove the enemy to their gunboats and fort, and held the town for ten hours ; captured many stores and horses; burned sixty bales of cotton, one steamer, and a dry-dock, bringing out fifty prisoners. My loss, as far as known, is twenty-five killed and wounded, among them Colonel A. P. Thompson."[343]

---

[337] Brian Steel Wills, *A Battle From the Start: The life of Nathan Bedford Forrest* (HarperPerennial, 1993), 136.

[338] Jack Hurst, *Nathan Bedford Forrest: A Biography* (Random House LLC, 1994), 150.

[339] Brian Steel Wills, *A Battle From the Start: The life of Nathan Bedford Forrest* (HarperPerennial, 1993), 165.

[340] John Allan Wyeth, *Life of Lieutenant-General Nathan Bedford Forrest* (New York: Harper & Brothers Publishers, 1908), 318.

[341] John Watson Morton, *The Artillery of Nathan Bedford Forrest's Cavalry: The Wizard of the Saddle* (Publishing House of the M. E. Church, South, Smith & Lamar, Agents, 1909), 156.

[342] Thomas Jordan, J. P. Pryor, *The Campaigns of Lieut.-Gen. N.B. Forrest, and of Forrest's Cavalry* (New Orleans, La.: Blelock & Company, 1868), 411.

[343] John Allan Wyeth, *Life of Lieutenant-General Nathan Bedford Forrest* (New

"There is a Federal force of five or six hundred at Fort Pillow, which I shall attend to in a day or two, as they have horses and supplies which we need."[344]

"MAJOR, The conduct of the officers and men garrisoning Fort Pillow has been such as to entitle them to being treated as prisoners of war. I demand the unconditional surrender of this garrison, promising you that you shall be treated as prisoners of war. My men have received a fresh supply of ammunition, and from their present position can easily assault and capture the fort. Should my demand be refused, I cannot be responsible for the fate of your command."[345]

"SIR, I have the honor to acknowledge the receipt of your note, asking one hour to consider my demand for your surrender. Your request cannot be granted. I will allow you twenty minutes from the receipt of this note for consideration; if at the expiration of that time the fort is not surrendered, I shall assault it. I do not demand the surrender of the gunboat."[346]

"SIR, My aide-de-camp, Captain Charles W. Anderson, is fully authorized to negotiate with you for the delivery of the wounded of the garrison at this place on board your vessel."[347]

"I know not how long we are to labor for that independence for which we have thus far struggled in vain, but this I do know, that I will never weary in defending our cause, which must ultimately succeed. Faith is the duty of the hour. We will succeed."[348]

"Taking with me my escort I moved rapidly to the rear. Lieutenant-Colonel Kelley being prevented from joining me as I had expected, I made the

---

York: Harper & Brothers Publishers, 1908), 330.

[344] James Harvey Mathes, *Great Commanders: General Forrest* (New York: D. Appleton & Company, 1902), 207.

[345] John Allan Wyeth, *Life of Lieutenant-General Nathan Bedford Forrest* (New York: Harper & Brothers Publishers, 1908), 344.

[346] Ibid., 349.

[347] Ibid., 357.

[348] Jack Hurst, *Nathan Bedford Forrest: A Biography* (Random House LLC, 1994), 229.

charge upon the enemy with my escort alone, producing a perfect stampede, capturing about fifty prisoners, twenty horses, and one ambulance." [349]

"This order was executed with a promptness and energy and gallantry which I have never seen excelled. The enemy was driven from his rifle-pits, and fled towards Spring Hill." [350]

"HEADQUARTERS FORREST S CAVALRY CORPS, GAINESVILLE, Alabama, May 9, 1865.
'SOLDIERS, *By an agreement made between Lieutenant-General Taylor, commanding the Department of Alabama, Mississippi, and East Louisiana, and Major-General Canby, commanding United States forces, the troops of this department have been surrendered. I do not think it proper or necessary at this time to refer to the causes which have reduced us to this extremity, nor is it now a matter of material consequence as to how such results were brought about. That we are beaten is a self-evident fact, and any further resistance on our part would be justly regarded as the very height of folly and rashness. The armies of Generals Lee and Johnston having surrendered, you are the last of all the troops of the Confederate States Army east of the Mississippi River to lay down your arms...."'* [351]

"*In 1871-72 General Forrest was summoned before the committee of Congress appointed to inquire into the condition of affairs in the late insurrectionary States in regard to the formation of the Kuklux organization. The committee stated that perhaps Generals Forrest and John B. Gordon knew more about the formation of this secret society than any others. Forrest testified that while he did not take an active part in the organization of the Kuklux, he knew that it was an association of citizens in his State (Tennessee) for self-protection. There was a great, widespread, and deep feeling of insecurity felt by those who had sympathized with the South in the war, as a result of Governor Brownlow's calling out the militia, and his*

---

[349] John Allan Wyeth, *Life of Lieutenant-General Nathan Bedford Forrest* (New York: Harper & Brothers Publishers, 1908), 536-537.
[350] John Watson Morton, *The Artillery of Nathan Bedford Forrest's Cavalry: The Wizard of the Saddle* (Publishing house of the M. E. Church, South, Smith & Lamar, agents, 1909), 156.
[351] John Allan Wyeth, *Life of Lieutenant-General Nathan Bedford Forrest* (New York: Harper & Brothers Publishers, 1908), 613.

proclamation they had interpreted as a license on the part of the State troops, without fear of punishment, to commit any kind of depredation against those lately in arms against the Union. Forrest stated that he had advised against all manner of violence on the part of the Southern people, and when the Loyal Leagues, for fear of the Kuklux, began to disband, he urged the disbanding of the other society."[352]

"Early in the summer of 1877, his faithful friend, Major Charles W. Anderson, was asked to visit him at Hurricane Springs, in middle Tennessee, where Forrest was spending the hot months in the hope that the waters would prove beneficial to his health. Major Anderson was quick to observe a softness of expression and a mildness of manner which he had not noticed in the trying times of war, and he must have shown something of surprise at this in his expression, for Forrest, as if reading his thought, said: 'Major, I am not the same man you were with so long and knew so well. I hope I am a better man now than then. I have been and am trying to lead another kind of life. Mary has been praying for me night and day for all these years, and I feel now that through her prayers my life has been spared and I have passed safely through so many dangers.'"[353]

Brigadier General Albert Pike

"There is a more laudable feeling also operating against us. We all love our common country. We love its Constitution, the Union and the flag of the United States. But commercial communities and legislative bodies are governed far more by considerations of sectional and local interest, than of a broad and catholic patriotism. We must not expect great commercial cities to aid in bringing about measures that shall divert the commerce of the world from them, by turning it into new channels, and build up other cities at their expense. It is not in human nature to do that which shall benefit another and injure one's self."[354]
"Pike's war song, 'Dixie...'"

---

[352] Ibid., 619.
[353] Ibid., 623.
[354] Fred W. Allsopp, *The Life Story of Albert Pike* (Parke-Harper, Audigier & Price, 1920), 69.

Soldiers of the Confederacy

Southrons, hear your country call you!
Up! lest worse than death befall you!
To arms! to arms! to arms! in Dixie!
Lo! all the beacon fires are lighted,
Let all your hearts be now united!
To arms! to arms! to arms! in Dixie!

Halt not till our Federation
Secures among Earth's powers its station!
To arms! to arms! to arms! in Dixie!
Then at peace, and crowned with glory,
Hear your children tell the story!
To arms! to arms! to arms! in Dixie!"[355]

"After the close of the War Between the States he wrote 'A Lament for Dixie,' consisting of nine verses, one of which reads,

Dear to us our conquered banners Greeted once with loud hosannas;
Dear the tattered flag of Dixie;
Dear the field of Honor glorious,
Where defeated or victorious,
Sleep the immortal Dead of Dixie."[356]

Lieutenant General Edmund Kirby-Smith

"I fear ours is to be no ordinary struggle. A settled determination to resist to the bitter end — with feelings inflamed and embittered by the outrages and vandalism's of the Northern people— will bring on a conflict in which, not only the laws and courtesies of war, but the common principles of humanity, will be cast to the wind."[357]

"Our men are poorly armed and equipped; the old altered flint lock musket is the chief arm that has been issued to them. One of the bad phases of States' Rights here exhibits itself. Each State in its sovereign capacity seized the arms,

---

[355] Ibid., 94.
[356] Ibid., 95.
[357] Arthur Howard, Noll, *General Kirby Smith* (Sewanee, Tennessee: The University Press at the University of the South, 1907), 170.

etc., in the forts, and arsenals within its limits. Instead of turning them over to the Confederate Government they appropriated them, at least the efficient ones, to their own use. "It is true, we make up in spirit and determination what we lack in means of defence. We feel our cause is just and Providence in His good time will bring it to a prosperous conclusion."[358]

"Stand by your colors, maintain your discipline. The great resources of this Department, its vast extent, the numbers, the discipline and efficiency of our army, will secure to our country terms that a proud people can with honor accept ; and may, under the providence of God, be the means of checking the triumph of our enemy and securing the final success of our cause."[359]

"Kentuckians — The Army of the Confederate States has again entered your territory under my command. Let no one make you believe that we come as invaders, to coerce your will or to exercise control over your soil. Far from it. The principle we maintain is, that government derives its just power from the consent of the governed. I shall enforce the strictest discipline in order that the property of citizens and non-combatants may be protected. I shall be compelled to procure subsistence for my troops among you, and this shall be paid for."[360]

"Kentuckians, we come not as invaders, but as liberators. We come in the spirit of your Resolutions of 1798. We come to arouse you from the lethargy which enshrouds your free thought, and forbodes the political death of your State. We come to test the truth of what we believe to be a foul aspersion that Kentuckians willingly join the attempt to subjugate us and deprive us of our property, our liberty, and our dearest rights. We come to strike off the chains which are riveted upon you. We call upon you to unite your arms and join with us in hurling back from our fair and sunny plains the Northern hordes which would deprive us of our liberty that they may enjoy our substance."[361]

---

[358] Ibid., 173.
[359] Ibid., 258.
[360] Ibid., 214.
[361] Ibid., 214-215.

Major General George Edward Pickett

"If Old Peter's nod means death, good-by, and God bless you, little one!"[362]

"I promised the little girl who is waiting and praying for me down in Virginia that I would keep fresh upon my lips until we should meet again the breath of the violets she gave me when we parted. Whatever my fate, Wilcox, I shall try to do my duty like a man, and I hope that, by that little girl's prayers, I shall to-day reach either glory or glory."[363]

"The hero of Gettysburg on both the northern and southern side was the private soldier."[364]

"I am humbly grateful, my little girl, for this loyal devotion which you give me—your Soldier. Let us pray to our dear Heavenly Father to spare us to each other and give us strength to bear cheerfully this enforced separation. I know that it cannot be long, and that sooner or later our flag will float over the seas of the world, for our cause is right and just."[365]

General Pierre Gustave Toutant Beauregard

"A reckless and unprincipled tyrant has invaded your soil. Abraham Lincoln, regardless of all moral, legal and constitutional restraints, has thrown his abolition hosts among you, who are murdering and imprisoning your citizens, confiscating and destroying your property, and committing other acts of violence and outrage too shocking and revolting to humanity to be enumerated. All rules of civilized warfare are abandoned, and they proclaim by their acts, if not on their banners, that their war cry is 'Beauty and Booty.' All that is dear to man—your honor and that of your wives and daughters—your fortunes and your lives are-involved in this momentous contest."[366]

---

[362] LaSalle Corbell Pickett, *Pickett and His Men* (Atlanta: The Foote and Davies Company, Printers and Binders, 1900), 301.
[363] Ibid., 302.
[364] Ibid., 281.
[365] *The Heart of a Soldier as Revealed in the Intimate Letters of Genl. George E. Pickett, CSA* (New York: Seth Moyle, 1913), 41.
[366] P. G. T. Beauregard, *A Proclamation. To the Good People of the Counties of Alexandria, Loudoun, Fairfax, and Prince William* (June 5, 1861, Alexandria,

Major General John Hunt Morgan

"Give me your pistol, my good fellow; I am Morgan." [367]

"My name is John Morgan, and my witnesses are 1,400 Confederate soldiers." [368]

Colonel John Singleton Mosby

"Our poor country has fallen a prey to the conqueror. The noblest cause ever defended by the sword is lost. The noble dead that sleep in their shallow though honored graves are far more fortunate than their survivors. I thought I had sounded the profoundest depth of human feeling, but this is the bitterest hour of my life." [369]

"My name is Mosby, and you are my prisoner." [370]

"Men, the Yankees are coming and it is very likely we will have a hard fight. When you are ordered to charge, I want you to go right through them. Reserve your fire until you get close enough to see clearly what you are shooting at, and then let every shot tell." [371]

"In one sense the charge that I did not fight fair is true. I fought for success and not for display. There was no man in the Confederate army who had less of the spirit of knight errantry in him, or who took a more practical view of war than I did." [372]

Virginia).

[367] Thomas F. Berry, *Four Years With Morgan and Forrest* (Harlow-Ratllff Company, 1914), 54.

[368] Mary Boykin Chesnut, *A Diary From Dixie* (New York: D. Appleton & Company, 1906), 209.

[369] Aristides Monteiro, *War Reminiscences By the Surgeon of Mosby's Command* (Richmond, Virginia, 1890), 129.

[370] Ibid., 38.

[371] James J. Williamson, *Mosby's Rangers: A Record of the Operations of the Forty-Third Battalion of Virginia Cavalry From Its Organization to the Surrender* (New York: Sturgis & Walton Company, 1909), 142.

[372] John Singleton Mosby, *Mosby's War Reminiscences, and Stuart's Cavalry Campaigns* (Dodd, Mead, 1887), 80.

"We lived on the country where we operated and drew nothing from Richmond except the gray jackets my men wore. We were mounted, armed, and equipped entirely off the enemy, but, as we captured a great deal more than we could use, the surplus was sent to supply Lee's army."[373]

"Lee was the most aggressive man I met in the war, and was always ready for an enterprise."[374]

Brigadier General Joseph Wheeler

"Much as I love the Union, and much as I am attached to my profession, all will be given up when my state, by its action, shows that such a course is necessary and proper If Georgia withdraws and becomes a separate state, I cannot with justice and propriety to my people, hesitate in resigning my commission."[375]

"Since the commencement of this sad war, I have used untiring exertions to maintain in my soldiers principles of chivalry and soldiery honor. They have been taught to spurn and despise the cowardly instincts which induce low men to frighten, abuse and rob defenseless women and children!"[376]

"Soldiers: The major-general commanding thanks his command for the energy and determined gallantry displayed in their recent operations. The foiling of a most stupendous effort on the part of the enemy to destroy our country is due to your valor and patriotism."[377]

Brigadier General Edward Porter Alexander

"As to the causes of the war, it will, of course, be understood that every former Confederate repudiates all accusations of treason or rebellion in the war, and even fighting to preserve the institution of slavery. The effort of the enemy to

---

[373] Charles Wells Russell, *The Memoirs of Colonel John S. Mosby* (Bloomington: Indiana University Press, 1959), 284.

[374] Ibid., 374.

[375] John Witherspoon DuBose, *General Joseph Wheeler And Army Of Tennessee* (New York: The Neale Publishing Company, 1912), 52.

[376] Ibid., 416.

[377] Ibid., 381.

destroy it without compensation was practical robbery, which, of course, we resisted. The unanimity and desperation of our resistance - even to the refusal of Lincoln's suggested compensation of Fortress Monroe, after the destruction had already occurred - clearly show our struggle to have been for that right of self-government which the Englishman has claimed, and fought for, as for nothing else, since the days of King John."[378]

Private Carlton McCarthy

"This banner, the witness and inspiration of many victories, which was proudly borne on every field from Manassas to Appomattox, was conceived on the field of battle, lived on the field of battle, and on the last fatal field ceased to have place or meaning in the world. But the men who followed it, and the world which watched its proud advance or defiant stand, see in it still the unstained banner of a brave and generous people, whose deeds have outlived their country, and whose final defeat but added luster to their grandest victories. It was not the flag of the Confederacy, but simply the banner, the battle-flag, of the Confederate soldier. As such it should not share in the condemnation which our cause received, or suffer from its downfall. The whole world can unite in a chorus of praise to the gallantry of the men who followed where this banner led."[379]

Brigadier General John Daniel Imboden

"I have no doubt thousands died at Andersonville in 1864, who would be living to-day if the United States had not declared medicines contraband of war, and by their close blockade of our coasts deprived us of an adequate supply of those remedial agents."[380]

---

[378] Edward Porter *Alexander, Military Memoirs of A Confederate: A Critical Narrative* (New York: Scribner's Sons, 1907), viii.

[379] Carlton McCarthy, *Detailed Minutiae of Soldier Life in the Army of Northern Virginia, 1861-1865* (Richmond: B. F. Johnson Publishing Company, 1882), 219.

[380] Spencer Tucker, *Brigadier General John D. Imboden: Confederate Commander in the Shenandoah* (University Press of Kentucky, 2010), 283.

Major John Pelham

"Ours is a just war, a holy cause. The invader must meet the fate he deserves and we must meet him as becomes us, as becomes men."[381]

Brigadier General Lewis A. Armistead

"Men, remember what you are fighting for. Remember your homes and your friends, your wives, mothers and sweethearts."[382]

Jackson's Chief of Staff Robert Lewis Dabney

"We have no need, sirs, to be ashamed of our dead; let us see to it that they be not ashamed of us."[383]

"It is to me simply incredible, that a people so shrewd and practical as those of the United States, should expect us to have discarded, through the logic of the sword merely, the convictions of a lifetime; or that they could be deceived by us, should we be base enough to assert it of ourselves. They know that the people of the South were conquered, and not convinced; and that the authority of the United States was accepted by us from necessity, and not from preference.... The people of the South went to war, because they sincerely believed (what their political fathers had taught them, with one voice, for two generations) that the doctrine of State-sovereignty for which they fought, was absolutely essential as the bulwark of the liberties of the people."[384]

---

[381] Jerry H. Maxwell, *The Perfect Lion: The Life and Death of Confederate Artillerist John Pelham* (University of Alabama Press, 2011), 61.

[382] Jeffry D. Wert, *Gettysburg, Day Three* (Simon and Schuster, 2002), 190-191.

[383] C. R. Vaughan, Editor, *Discussions By Robert Lewis Dabney, Volume 4* (Mexico, Mo.: Crescent Book House, 1897), 120.

[384] Robert Louis Dabney, *Life and Campaigns of Lieut.-Gen. Thomas J. Jackson* (New York: Blelock & Company, 1866), viii-ix.

Captain Robert Tansil

"In entering the public service, I took an oath to support the Constitution, which necessarily gives me the right to interpret it. Our institutions, according to my understanding, are founded upon the principle and right of self-government. The States, in forming the Confederacy (in 1783) did not relinquish that right, and I believe that each State has a clear and unquestionable right to secede whenever the people thereof think proper, and the Federal Government has no legal or moral authority to use physical force to keep them in the Union. Entertaining these views, I cannot conscientiously join in a war against any of the States which have already seceded or may hereafter secede, either North or South, for the purpose of coercing them back into the Union."[385]

Brigadier General Roger Weightman Hanson

"Forward—forward, my brave boys, to the charge!"[386]

"I am willing to die with such a wound, received in so glorious a cause."[387]

Corporal Sam R. Watkins

"The South is our country; the North is the country of those who live there. We are an agricultural people; they are a manufacturing people. They are the descendants of the good old Puritan Plymouth Rock stock, and we of the South from the proud and aristocratic stock of Cavaliers. We believe in the doctrine of State Rights, they in the doctrine of centralization."[388]

---

[385] John Thomas Scharf, *History of the Confederate States Navy from Its Organization to the Surrender of Its Last Vessel* (Rogers & Sherwood, 1887), 769.

[386] William Parker Snow, *Southern Generals, Their Lives and Campaigns* (New York: Charles B. Richardson, 1866), 355.

[387] William Terrell Lewis, *Genealogy of the Lewis Family in America: From the Middle of the Seventeenth Century Down to the Present Time* (Louisville: The Courier-Journal Job Printing Company), 170.

[388] *Co. Aytch, Maury Grays, First Tennessee Regiment; or A Side Show of the Big Show* (Chattanooga, Tennessee: Times Printing Company, 1900), 13.

Sergeant Eli Pinson Landers

"I want my body taken up and laid in the dust around old Sweetwater and I want a tombstone put at my head with my name and my company and regiment, the day I enlisted and the name and date of the battles I have ever been in."[389]

Major Reuben Everett Wilson

"If I ever disown, repudiate, or apologize for the Cause for which Lee fought and Jackson died, let the lightnings of Heaven rend me, and the scorn of all good men and true women be my portion. Sun, Moon, Stars, all fall on me when I cease to love the Confederacy. 'Tis the cause, not the fate of the Cause, that is glorious!"[390]

Brigadier General Benjamin McCulloch

"Come, my brave lads, I have a battery for you to charge and the day is ours."[391]

Brigadier General Barnard Bee

"Let us determine to die here, and we will conquer."[392]

Major General Daniel Harvey Hill

"We are in the hands of God and as safe on the battlefield as anywhere else. We will be exposed to a heave fire, but the arm of God is mightier than the artillery of the enemy."[393]

---

[389] Elizabeth Whitley Roberson, *Weep Not for Me, Dear Mother* (Pelican Publishing, 1996), 120-121.

[390] Michael Andrew Grissom, *Southern by the Grace of God* (Pelican Publishing, 1989), 164.

[391] Victor M. Rose, *The Life and Services of General Benjamin Bullouch* (Philadelphia: Pictorial Bureau, 1888), 140.

[392] Shelby Foote, *The Civil War: A Narrative: Volume 1: Fort Sumter to Perryville* (New York: Random House, 1958), 78.

[393] W. J. Peele, *Lives of Distinguished North Carolinians* (The North Carolina

Colonel Richard Henry Lee

"It is stated in books and papers that Southern children read and study that all the blood shedding and destruction of property of that conflict was because the South rebelled without cause against the best government the world ever saw; that although Southern soldiers were heroes in the field, skillfully massed and led, they and their leaders were rebels and traitors who fought to overthrow the Union, and to preserve human slavery, and that their defeat was necessary for free government and the welfare of the human family. As a Confederate soldier and as a citizen of Virginia, I deny the charge, and denounce it as a calumny. We were not rebels; we did not fight to perpetuate human slavery, but for our rights and privileges under a government established over us by our fathers and in defense of our homes."[394]

Colonel Alfred Marmaduke Hobby

To the Memory of Col. Thos S. Lubbock

Who died in Nashville, Tenn., January 9, 1862, while in the service of his country, commanding the Terry Rangers.

"Drape in gloom our Southern ensign! gently fold its crimson bars,
While cypress wreaths around it twine, and dim with: ears its burning stars:
Hearts are throbbing, eyes are weeping tears on noble Lubbock's grave
Calm in death his form is sleeping—lamented LUBBOCK—true and brave!

But yesterday, the minute gun came booming on our shore,
And on our day a shadow hung—brave Terry was no more!
He died on the soil that gave him birth, defending his country's trust;
Our vandal foes he crush'd to earth, like servile worms of dust.

Our Lubbock! unto thee we turn'd to lead our Texian band;
We knew what fires within thee burn'd, what courage nerv'd thy hand:
We felt that thou would'st win from fame a laurel wreath of glory;
And deeds of valor give thy name high place in Southern story.

Publishing Society, 1898), 533.

[394] Timothy S. Sedore, *An Illustrated Guide to Virginia's Confederate Monuments* (SIU Press, April 29, 2011), 10.

When years ago, a single Star illumed our Western sky.
Its radiant beams were hail'd afar, and caught his beaming eye
Forsaking home to aid the brave—foes and danger scorning—
To his adopted mother gave the vigor of life's morning.

Where'er her ensign was unfurl'd, beneath were souls to dare.
And valor's arm foes backward hurl'd in victory's meteor glare;
He saw it wave, that Lone Star Flag, above the Rocky Mountains,
Where frozen tears from the icy crag weep into silver fountains.
He saw that flag reflected gleam down deep in Pecos river.
Its azure folds, its silv'ry sheen on flowing waters quiver:

He saw it meet the rising day on Santa Fe's broa'd plain,
Which, cold and cheerless, stretch'd away where gloom and silence reign.
He saw that star the heavens climb through battle's lurid light.
Still upward in its strength sublime, unutterably bright;
In Aztec's dungeons, dark and deep, its beams resplendent shedding,
He heard success, along fame's steep, our mystic future treading.

Unchanging still thro' rest or toil, his heart for Texas burning,
It lov'd her sons, and blood-bought soil, it knew no shade of turning;
And when our honor was assail'd, indignant shouts were rais'd—
The Lone Star flutter'd in the gale, and redden'd, flashed and blaz'd.

It swept on high the fleecy cloud, it sought a loftier station,
And join'd, 'midst cheers of freemen loud, the Southern constellation;
And there it shines—GOD bless that star !—God bless her sister stars!
'Tis Venus in the days of peace—in war the blood red Mars!

Upon Manassas' gory field, where fell the shafts of death,
Its new-born splendor stood reveal'd, 'midst sulphurous breath—
Where thickest rain'd war's iron hail, and gush'd the crimson tide.
Undaunted there our Lubbock stood, brave Terby by his side.

Far in advance on Fairfax Heights, rais'd by a tyrant's minion,
They struck the flag that dared insult our honor'd Old Dominion;
Enough ! they were strong friends in youth, in spring-time's pleasant
weather—

Two soul's close bound in bonds of truth—in death they sleep together.

Time's brightest page their names adorn, their deeds are history's trust.
And fame's green laurel, fresh as morn, will crown their honor'd busts;
The fever'd frame and aching head of Lubbock is at rest—
He sleepeth well, 'neath Southern skies, still looking to the West

Proud Carolina ne'er has borne a truer son, or braver,
And, like herself, lie trampled on power's threat or favor —
But pulseless lies that heart of worth beneath the swelling sod;
His body with its mother earth, his spirit with its God!

Our hearts bereav'd, a pall is cast, and wither'd seem life's
flowers; O let your tears flow free and fast—with them shall mingle ours;
Eternal honor to the brave! may spring her garlands wreathe
Immortal blooms to deck his grave, and Christ his soul receive"[395]

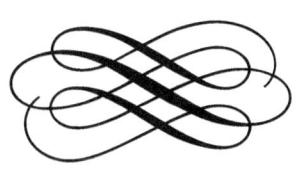

---

[395] Francis D. Allan, *Allan's Lone Star ballads: A Collection of Southern Patriotic Songs, Made During Confederate Times* (Galveston: J. D. Sawyer Publisher, 1874), 148-150.

Women of the Confederacy

Cornelia Peake McDonald	Ella King Newsom
Cornelia Phillips Spencer	Florence May Porter
Eliza Frances Andrews	Mary Anna Jackson
Isabelle "Belle" Boyd	Augusta J. Kollock
Judith White McGuire	Leora Sims
Loretta Janeta Velasquez	Kate Cumming
Mary Ann Harris Gay	Betty Herndon Maury
Mary Boykin Chesnut	Lucy Smith
Rose O'Neal Greenhow	Sarah Lois Wadley
Sarah Morgan Dawson	Cordelia Lewis Scales
Varina Howell Davis	Mary Ann Loughborough
Susan Blanchard Elder	Marie Ravenel De La Coste
Susan Bradford	Mary Byson
Mary Darby de Treville	Virginia McCollum Stinson

"Politically I did not like Mr. Lincoln, for in him I saw the destroyer. As long as it served his purpose, Mr. Lincoln boldly advocated the right of Secession."[396]
Belle Boyd

Cornelia Peake McDonald

"Had I forgotten the gallant array and brave appearance of Gen. Johnston's army as they passed our house on their march to their great victory at Manassas? The exulting strains of 'Dixie' or the 'Bonnie Blue Flag' almost giving wings to their feet as they moved triumphantly on, keeping step to the joyous music."[397]

Cornelia Phillips Spencer

"Southerners can not write calmly of such scenes yet. Their houses were turned into seraglios, every portable article of value, plate, china and glassware, provisions and books were carried off, and the remainder destroyed; hundreds of carriages and vehicles of all kinds were burned in piles; where houses were isolated they were burned; women were grossly insulted, and robbed of clothing and jewelry; nor were darker and nameless tragedies wanting in lonely situations. No; they hardly dare trust themselves to think of these things. 'That way lies madness.' But the true story of 'The Great March' will yet be written."[398]

"One of the first of General Sherman's own acts, after his arrival, was of peculiar hardship. One of the oldest and most venerable citizens of the place, with a family of sixteen or eighteen children and grandchildren, most of

---

[396] Belle Boyd, *Belle Boyd In Camp and Prison, Vol. 2* (London: Saunders, Otley and Company, 1865), 273.
[397] Katharine M. Jones, *Heroines Of Dixie Confederate: Women Tell Their Story Of The War* (New York: The Bobbs-Merrill Company, Inc., 1955), 100.
[398] Cornelia Phillips Spencer, *The Last Ninety Days of the War in North Carolina* (New York: Watchman Publishing Company, 1866), 51.

them females, was ordered, on a notice of a few hours, to vacate his house, for the convenience of the General himself, which of course was done. The gentleman was nearly eighty years of age, and in very feeble health. The outhouses, fences, grounds, etc., were destroyed, and the property greatly damaged during its occupation by the General. Not a farm-house in the country but was visited and wantonly robbed. Many were burned, and very many, together with out-houses, were pulled down and hauled into camps for use. Generally not a live animal, not a morsel of food of any description was left, and in many instances not a bed or sheet or change of clothing for man, woman, or child. It was most heart-rending to see daily crowds of country people, from three-score and ten years of age, down to the unconscious infant carried in its mother's arms, coming into the town to beg food and shelter, to ask shelter from those who had despoiled them. Many of these families lived for days on parched corn, on peas boiled in water without salt, on scraps picked about the camps. The number of carriages, buggies, and wagons brought in is almost incredible. They kept for their own use what they wished, and burned or broke up the rest."[399]

Eliza Frances Andrews

"I used to have some Christian feeling towards Yankees, but now that they have invaded our country and killed so many of our men and desecrated so many homes, I can't believe that when Christ said " Love your enemies," he meant Yankees. Of course I don't want their souls to be lost, for that would be wicked ... "[400]

Isabelle "Belle" Boyd

"If it is a crime to love the South, its cause, and its President, then I am a criminal. I am in your power; do with me as you please. But I fear you not, I would rather lie down in this prison and die, than leave it owing allegiance to such a government as yours."[401]

---

[399] Ibid., 95-96.
[400] Eliza Frances Andrews, *The War-Time Journal of a Georgia Girl, 1864-1865* (D. Appleton & Company, 1808), 149.
[401] Louis A. Sigaud, *Belle Boyd Confederate Spy* (Richmond: The Dietz Press, Incorporated, 1945), 80.

"The secession of the Southern States, individually or in the aggregate, was the certain consequence of Mr. Lincoln's election. His accession to a power supreme and almost unparalleled was an unequivocal declaration, by the merchants of New England, that they had resolved to exclude the landed proprietors of the South from all participation in the legislation of their common country."[402]

"Acting upon General Jackson's advice, I removed to Winchester; and it was there and then that I received my commission as Captain and honorary Aide-de-camp to 'Stonewall' Jackson; and thenceforth I enjoyed the respect paid to an officer by soldiers."[403]

Judith White McGuire

"The body lies in state to-day at the Capitol, wrapped in the Confederate flag, and literally covered with lilies of the valley and other beautiful Spring flowers. To-morrow the sad cortege will wend its way to Lexington, where he will be buried, according to his dying request, in the "Valley of Virginia. As a warrior, we may appropriately quote from Byron: 'His spirit wraps the dusky mountain, His memory sparkles o'er the fountain, The meanest rill, the mightiest river, Rolls mingling with his name forever.' As a Christian, in the words of St. Paul, I thank God to be able to say, 'He has fought the good fight, he has finished his course, he has kept the faith. Henceforth there is laid up for him a crown of righteousness, which the Lord, the righteous Judge, shall give him at the last day.'"[404]

"June 15, 1861—Yesterday was set apart by the President as a day of prayer and fasting, and I trust that throughout the Confederacy the blessing of God was invoked upon the army and country."[405]

---

[402] Belle Boyd, *Belle Boyd In Camp and Prison, Vol. 1* (London: Saunders, Otley and Company, 1865), 44.
[403] Katharine M. Jones, *Heroines Of Dixie Confederate: Women Tell Their Story Of The War* (New York: The Bobbs-Merrill Company, Inc., 1955), 174.
[404] Judith White McGuire, *Diary Of A Southern Refugee, During The War By A Lady Of Virginia* (New York: E. J. Hale & Son, 1867), 212.
[405] Ibid., 29-30.

"It is said that our new steamer, the 'Tallahassee,' has been within sixty miles of the city of New York, very much to the terror of the citizens. It also destroyed six large vessels. I bid it God-speed with all my heart; I want the North to feel the war to its core, and then it will end, and not before."[406]

"In the Valley of Virginia an immense amount of private property has been destroyed. Sheridan, glorying in his shame, boasts of, and probably magnifies, what has been done in that way. He telegraphs to Grant that he has burned 2,000 barns. The Lord shorten his dreadful work, and have mercy upon the sufferers!"[407]

"How many young spirits have fled—how many bleeding, breaking hearts have been left upon earth, from the sanguinary work of this summer! Grant still remains near Petersburg; still by that means is he besieging Richmond. He has been baffled at all points, and yet his indomitable perseverance knows no bounds. Sherman still besieges Atlanta. God help us!"[408]

"November, 1864— The war news seems encouraging. Many persons are very despondent, but I do not feel so—perhaps I do not understand the military signs. Our men below Richmond have certainly had many successes of late. Sheridan, instead of capturing Lynchburg, as he promised, is retreating down the Valley. In the South, the army of Tennessee is in Sherman's rear, and Forrest still carries everything before him. General Price seems to be doing well in Missouri; Arkansas and Texas seem to be all right. Kentucky, too, (poor Kentucky!) seems more hopeful. Then why should we despond? Maryland, alas for Maryland! the tyrant's heel appears too heavy for her, and we grievously fear that the prospect of her union with the South is rapidly passing away."[409]

Loretta Janeta Velasquez

"For the part I took in the great contest between the South and the North I have no apologies to offer. I did what I thought to be right…[410]

---

[406] Ibid., 292.
[407] Ibid., 314.
[408] Ibid., 293.
[409] Ibid., 316.
[410] C.J. Worthington, Editor, *The Woman In Battle: A Narrative of the Ex-*

"Gentlemen, here's to the success of our young Confederacy."[411]

Mary Ann Harris Gay

"With the placid waters of that ever flowing stream, in the name of the Southern Confederacy, I christened one of the best friends I ever had 'Johnny Reb,' a name ever dear to me."[412]

"And by this order, and by others even more oppressive and diabolical, the Nero of the nineteenth century, alias William Tecumseh Sherman, was put upon record as the born leader of the most ruthless, Godless band of men ever organized in the name of patriotism—a band which, but for a few noble spirits, who, by the power of mind over matter, exerted a restraining influence, would not have left a Southerner to tell the tale of its fiendishness on its route to the sea."[413]

"The long tramp to the Stone Mountain was very lonely. Not a living thing overtook or passed us, and we soon crossed over the line and entered a war-stricken section of country where stood chimneys only, where lately were pretty homes and prosperity, now departed. Ah, those chimneys standing amid smouldering ruins! No wonder they were called 'Sherman's sentinels,' as they seemed to be keeping guard over those scenes of desolation. The very birds of the air and beasts of the field had fled to other sections."[414]

"Callous indeed would have been the heart who could have gone merrily over that devastated, impoverished land. Sherman, with his destructive hosts, had been there, and nothing remained within the conquered boundary upon which "Sheridan's Crow" could have subsisted."[415]

---

ploits, Adventure, and Travels of Madame Loretta Janeta Velasquez, Otherwise Known As Harry T. Buford, Confederate States Army (Hartford: T. Belknap, 1876), 606.

[411] Ibid., 54.
[412] Mary Ann Harris Gay, *Life in Dixie During the War 1863-1864-1865* (Atlanta: Constitutional Job Office, 1892), 199.
[413] Ibid., 126.
[414] Ibid., 163.
[415] Ibid., 194-195.

"Much as I enjoyed this luxurious home, and its refined appointments, there was a controlling motive—a nearer tie—that made me willing to again take up the hardships and perils of warfare, and battle for life with that relentless enemy left by Sherman to complete his cruel work, the aforesaid General Starvation."[416]

"In vain did I look round for relief? There was nothing left in the country to eat. Yea, a crow flying over it would have failed to discover a morsel with which to appease its hunger; for a Sheridan by another name had been there with his minions of destruction, and had ruthlessly destroyed every vestige of food and every means of support."[417]

"... I took a seat by my mother on the front door steps and engaged in a pleasant conversation with a group of young Federal soldiers, who seemed much attached to us, and with whom I conversed with unreserved candor, and often expressed regret that they were in hostile array towards a people who had been goaded to desperation by infringement upon constitutional rights by those who had pronounced the only ligament that bound the two sections of the country together, "a league with hell, and a covenant with the devil." This I proved to them by documents published at the North, and by many other things of which they were ignorant."[418]

Mary Boykin Chesnut

Final words, August 2, 1865: "Never let me hear that the blood of the brave has been shed in vain! No; it sends a cry down through all time."[419]

"General Grant is charmed with Sherman's successful movements; says he has destroyed millions upon millions of our property in Mississippi. I hope that may not be true, and that Sherman may fail as Kilpatrick did. Now, if we still had Stonewall or Albert Sidney Johnston where Joe Johnston and Polk are, I would not give a fig for Sherman's chances."[420]

---

[416] Ibid., 235.
[417] Ibid., 218.
[418] Ibid., 131.
[419] Mary Boykin Chesnut, *A Diary From Dixie* (New York: D. Appleton & Company, 1906), 404.
[420] Ibid., 299.

"If Albert Sidney Johnston had lived! Poor old General Lee has no backing. Stonewall would have saved us from Antietam. Sherman will now catch General Lee by the rear, while Grant holds him by the head, and while Hood and Thomas are performing an Indian war-dance on the frontier. Hood means to cut his way to Lee; see if he doesn't. The Yanks have had a struggle for it. More than once we seemed to have been too much for them. We have been so near to success it aches one to think of it. So runs the table-talk."[421]

Rose O'Neal Greenhow

"Many who were dear to me have been slain, or maimed for life, fighting in defence of all that makes life of value. Instead of friends, I see in those statesmen of Washington only mortal enemies. Instead of loving and worshipping the old flag of the stars and stripes, I see in it only the symbol of murder, plunder, oppression, and shame! and, like every other faithful Confederate, I dwell with delight on the many glorious fields where this dishonoured standard has gone down before the stainless battleflag of the Confederacy."[422]

"I have been now nearly eight months a prisoner. I am not prepared to say whether I will appear before you in your capacity of commissioner. I deny the power of your Government lawfully to deprive me of my legal rights. And as to that old flag—there was a time when I looked upon it as the proudest emblem of human freedom on earth, and have in other lands bowed before it in holy reverence; but now there is no pirate flag that floats upon the sea which is not more honourable in my eye, for none covers such infamy."[423]

"I was under intense excitement, for, after nearly ten weary months of imprisonment, I was in sight of the promised land. In a short time we reached the shore, and my foot pressed the sacred soil. I had worn ton my shoulders from Fortress Monroe, in the folds of a shawl, a large battle-flag, which had been made by myself and other prisoners whilst in prison for

---

[421] Ibid., 331.
[422] Rose Greenhow, *My Imprisonment and the First Year of Abolition Rule at Washington* (London: Richard Bentley, Publisher in Ordinary to Her Majesty, 1863), 4.
[423] Ibid., 261-262.

General Beauregard. I felt strongly tempted to unfold it and cast it to the breeze, as a parting penance to the Yankees; but I remembered that the same means might be useful again."[424]

Sarah Morgan Dawson

"Dreadful news has come of the defeat of Lee at Gettysburg. Think I believe it all? He may have been defeated; but no one of these reports of total overthrow and rout do I credit. Yankees jubilant, Southerners dismal. Brother, with principles on one side and brothers on the other, is correspondingly distracted."[425]

"Thursday the 13th came the dreadful tidings of the surrender of Lee and his army on the 9th. Everybody cried, but I would not, satisfied that God will still save us, even though all should apparently be lost."[426]

"While praying for the return of those who have fought so nobly for us, how I have dreaded their first days at home! Since the boys died, I have constantly thought of what pain it would bring to see their comrades return without them - to see families reunited, and know that ours never could be again, save in heaven."[427]

"I devote all my red, white, and blue silk to the manufacture of Confederate flags. As soon as one is confiscated, I make another, until my ribbon is exhausted, when I will sport a duster emblazoned in high colors, "Hurra! for the Bonny blue flag!" Henceforth, I wear one pinned to my bosom — not a duster, but a little flag; the man who says take it off will have to pull it off for himself; the man who dares attempt it — well! a pistol in my pocket fills up the gap. I am capable, too."[428]

---

[424] Ibid., 321.
[425] Sarah Morgan Dawson, *A Confederate Girl's Diary* (New York: Houghton Mifflin Company, 1913), 399.
[426] Ibid., 435.
[427] Ibid., 439.
[428] Ibid., 24.

Susan Blanchard Elder

THE CONFEDERATE FLAG

Bright banner of freedom, with pride I unfold thee.
Fair flag of my country with love I behold thee;
Gleaming above us, in freshness and youth.
Emblem of liberty symbol of truth.
For this flag of my country in triumph shall wave
O'er the Southerner's home and the Southerner's grave.

All bright are the stars that are beaming upon us,
And bold are the bars that are gleaming above us,
The one shall increase in their number and light;
The other grows bolder in power and might
For this flag of my country in triumph shall wave.
O'er the Southerner's home or the Southerner's grave.

Those bars of bright red shows our firm resolution.
To die if need be, shielding thee from pollution;
For man in this hour must give all he holds dear,
And woman her prayer and words of high cheer
If they wish this fair banner in triumph to wave,
O'er the Southerner's home and the Southerner's grave.

To the great God of battle we look in reliance;
On our fierce Northern foe with contempt and defiance;
For the South shall smile on in fragrance and bloom;
When the North is fast sinking in silence and gloom
For the flag of our country in triumph must wave
O'er the Southerner's home or the Southerner's grave. [429]

---

[429] Susan Blanchard Elder, *The Confederate Flag* (Blackmar & Brothers, 1861).

Varina Howell Davis

"Under it [the Battle Flag] we won our victories and its glory will never fade. It is enshrined in our hearts forever."[430]

Susan Bradford

"January 8, 1861— ... Mr. Sanderson was very interesting. He recounted the rights which the states retained when they delegated other rights to the general government in the Constitution. He made it so perfectly clear that all and every state had the right to withdraw from the Union, if her rights and liberty were threatened. He said the Committee on Ordinances had carefully examined into the question and they could find no reason why Florida should not exercise her right to withdraw from a compact, which now threatened her with such dire disaster."[431]

Unknown Southern Woman

"I mourn the death of my husband, but my greatest regret is that none of his sons are old enough to take his place to battle for our liberties."[432]

Mary Darby de Treville

"You should have seen us last night, all sitting around one big camp fire, a great many soldiers with us, all singing 'The Bonnie Blue Flag,' 'Dixie,' 'My Maryland,' and many others. The soldiers did enjoy the singing. Some of them said: 'It is you women who made us soldiers fight and never give up. God bless and protect our women. Three cheers for them!' which they gave

---

[430] Varina Howell, *Jefferson Davis, Ex-President of the Confederate States of America: A Memoir, Volume 2* (New York: Belford Company, Publishers, 1890), 36.

[431] Katharine M. Jones, *Heroines Of Dixie Confederate: Women Tell Their Story Of The War* (New York: The Bobbs-Merrill Company, Inc., 1955), 8.

[432] H. W. E. Jackson, *The Southern Women of the Second American Revolution, Their Trials & Yankee Barbarity Illustrated, Our Naval Victories and Exploits of Confederate War Steamers, Captures Yankee Gunboats* (Atlanta, Georgia: Intelligencer Steam-Power Press, 1863), 16.

with heartfelt fervor. As far as you could see there were camp fires all around."[433]

Ella King Newsom

"I got to know General Hardee better than any others of our distinguished Generals and always found him manly and a splendid soldier though almost womanly in the caring for his troops."[434]

Florence May Porter

"One gloriously bright day in the spring of 1861 there gathered in the little town of Plattsburg, Mo., a large and enthusiastic concourse of people, drawn together by a unity of purpose and principle, the giving of outward expression of their sympathy with the more southern states in their contention for 'states' rights.' The occasion was one of great moment to the citizens of the town, county, state, and in fact, to the entire South, in as much as it tended to express the inclination and will of the mass of the people of our own Missouri."[435]

Mary Anna Jackson

"About the dawn of that Sabbath morning, April 21, 1861, our door-bell rang, and the order came that Major Jackson should bring the cadets to Richmond immediately. Without waiting for breakfast, he repaired at once to the Institute, to make arrangements as speedily as possible for marching, but finding that several hours of preparation would necessarily be required, he appointed the hour for starting at one o'clock P.M. He sent a message to his pastor, Dr. White, requesting him to come to the barracks and offer a prayer with the command before its departure."[436]

---

[433] *South Carolina Women in the Confederacy, Volume 2* (Columbia, S.C.: The State Company, 1907), 187.

[434] J. Fraise Richard, *The Florence Nightingale of the Southern Army; Experiences of Mrs. Ella K. Newsom, Confederate Nurse in the Great War of 1861-65* (New York: Broadway Publishing Company, 1914), 64.

[435] *Reminiscences of the Women of Missouri During the Sixties* (Missouri Division, United Daughters of the Confederacy: 1920), 10.

[436] Katharine M. Jones, *Heroines Of Dixie Confederate: Women Tell Their Story*

"On Sunday morning [May 3, 1863], as we arose from family worship in Dr. Hoge's parlor, Dr. Brown informed me that the news had come that General Jackson had been wounded. ... On Tuesday my brother Joseph arrived to my great relief, to take me to my husband, but my disappointment was only increased by his report that it had taken him nearly three days to ride through the country and elude the raiding enemy. It was not until Thursday morning that the blockade was broken, and we went up on an armed train prepared to fight its way through.

A few hours of unmolested travel brought us to Guiney's Station, and we were taken at once to the residence of Mr. Chandler, which was a large country-house, and very near it, in the yard, was a small, humble abode, in which lay my precious, suffering husband.

From the time I reached him he was too ill to notice or talk much, and he lay most of the time in a semi-conscious state; but when aroused, he recognized those about him and consciousness would return. Soon after I entered his room he was impressed by the woeful anxiety and sadness betrayed in my face, and said: 'My darling, you must cheer up, and not wear a long face.... My darling, you are very much loved.'

Early on Sunday morning, the 10th of May, I was called out of the sick-room by Dr. Morrison, who told me that the doctors, having done everything that human skill could devise to stay the hand of death, had lost all hope, and that my precious, brave, noble husband could not live!"[437]

Augusta J. Kollock

"The whole city has been wild with excitement ever since Sumter was taken, and has just begun to get a little quiet, but I suppose we must prepare for hot times now, that is if the Federal Government persists in the insane policy of coercion. It is the most absurd thing I ever heard of, and I rather think if they attempt it, they will find to their cost, that it is not quite so easy to subdue us as they fancied."[438]

Of The War (New York: The Bobbs-Merrill Company, Inc., 1955), 22.
[437] Ibid., 219.
[438] Ibid., 11.

Leora Sims

"Virginia, the home of our loved Washington, the resting place of many great and noble, has been laid waste, and in the midst of the true and gallant, we find, thickly woven, traitors and Yankees of the blackest dye, if that race will admit of comparison. I cannot realize that our loved Carolina is now the abiding place of our enemies. You have the invaders at Cape Hatteras and we at Port Royal. Our people have acted nobly; some cotton has fallen into the hands of the enemy; and for my part, and it is so with nearly everyone in this state we would rather have lost our men, than that the Yankees should have been gratified."[439]

Kate Cummings

"April 17, 1862—I was going round as usual this morning, washing the faces of the men, and had got half through with one before I found out that he was dead. He was lying on the gallery by himself, and had died with no one near him. These are terrible things...."[440]

"April 23, 1862— A young man whom I have been attending is going to have his arm cut off. Poor fellow! I am doing all I can to cheer him. He says that he knows that he will die, as all who have had limbs amputated in this hospital have died."[441]

Betty Herndon Maury

"Easter Sunday April 20, 1862—We can see the Yankees and their tents across the river. They received a reinforcement of ten thousand last night. One can scarcely realize that the enemy is so near and that we are in their hands. I heard the Yankees this evening with their full brass band playing 'Yankee Doodle' and 'The Star Spangled Banner.' I could not realize that they were enemies and invaders. The old tunes brought back recollections of the old love for them. It was a sad and painful feeling."[442]

---

[439] Ibid., 69-70.
[440] Ibid., 114.
[441] Ibid., 116.
[442] Ibid., 118.

"General Stuart made a most daring dash the other day with two thousand of our Cavalry. They passed through the enemy lines to their rear, burnt several loaded transports on the Pamunky and many loaded wagons, took many horses and mules and prisoners. We lost one man killed and two wounded and were gone between two and three days. They were greeted with shouts and cheers by the country people as they galloped along. One old woman rushed out to her gate and shouted out above all the clatter and din, 'Hurrah, my Dixie boys, you drive the blue coated varmints away.'"[443]

"On the 13th of December God blessed us with a great victory at Fredericksburg. Upwards of eighteen thousand of the enemy were killed. We lost but one thousand. Even the Yankees acknowledge it to be a terrible defeat. The battle took place in and around the town. The streets were strewn with the fallen enemy. The houses were broken open, sacked, and used for hospitals and their dead were buried in almost every yard."[444]

Lucy Smith

"It is with great emotion that we women of the Southern Confederacy and striving to maintain ourselves as patriotic mothers are almost driven to subjugation and almost preferring the tyranny of Lincoln to the tantalizing inhumane treatment to our soldiers by our head leading Generals and regimental surgeons."[445]

Sarah Lois Wadley

"Friday-Dec. 26th, 1862—Our turn has come at last. We heard this morning the Yankees had come as far as Delhi (on the railroad) burning everything in their track, and coming four miles an hour. We know nothing of their force, all suppose that they are coming to Monroe. I do not know whether our few troops will resist or not. Willie is gone in at full speed to ascertain the truth of the matter and to bring back our teams which went in this morning for corn. Oh if Father was here! I am determined, come what may, never to renounce my country, but what is before us!"[446]

---

[443] Ibid., 151.
[444] Ibid., 197-198.
[445] Ibid., 166.
[446] Ibid., 196.

Cordelia Lewis Scales

"Oh! how I did shout when Vandorn came into Holly Springs. He made them "skeedaddle" shows you born. I was so glad I had the pleasure of seeing Mr. Yankee run; just the day before some of them asked me where our men were that they could not find any of them."[447]

Emma Sansom

"We were at home on the morning of May 2, 1863, when about eight or nine o'clock, a company of men wearing blue uniforms and riding mules and horses galloped past the house and went on towards the bridge. Pretty soon a great crowd of them came along, and some of them stopped at the gate and asked us to bring them some water. Sister and I each took a bucket of water, and gave it to them at the gate. One of them asked me where my father was. I told him he was dead. He asked me if I had any brothers. I told him I had six. He asked where they were, and I said they were in the Confederate Army. 'Do they think the South will whip?' 'They do.' 'What do you think about it?' 'I think God is on our side and we will win.' 'You do? Well, if you had seen us whip Colonel Roddey the other day and run him across the Tennessee River, you would have thought God was on the side of the best artillery.'"[448]

Mary Ann Loughborough

"What a sad evening we spent continually hearing of friends and acquaintances left dead on the field, or mortally wounded, and being brought in ambulances to the hospital! We almost feared to retire that night; no one seemed to know whether the Federal army was advancing or not; some told us that they were many miles away, and others that they were quite near. How did we know but in the night we might be -awakened by the tumult of their arrival!"[449]

---

[447] Ibid., 207.
[448] Ibid., 215-216.
[449] Ibid., 227.

Marie Ravenel De La Coste

"Somebody's Darling

Into a ward of the whitewashed walls
Where the dead and the dying lay—
Wounded by bayonets, shells, and balls—
Somebody's darling was borne one day.
Somebody's darling! so young and so brave,
Wearing still on his pale, sweet face
Soon to be hid by the dust of the grave—
The lingering light of his boyhood's grace.

Matted and damp are the curls of gold
Kissing the snow of that fair young brow;
Pale are the lips of delicate mould—
Somebody's darling is dying now.
Back from the beautiful blue-veined brow
Brush the wandering waves of gold;
Cross his hands on his bosom now—
Somebody's darling is still and cold.

Kiss him once for Somebody's sake;
Murmur a prayer, soft and low;
One bright curl from the cluster take—
They were Somebody's pride, you know.
Somebody's hand hath rested there;
Was it a mother's, soft and white?
And have the lips of a sister fair
Been baptized in those waves of light?

God knows best. He has Somebody's love;
Somebody's heart enshrined him there;
Somebody wafted his name above,
Night and morn, on the wings of prayer.
Somebody wept when he marched away.
Looking so handsome, brave, and grand;
Somebody's kiss on his forehead lay;
Somebody clung to his parting hand;—

Somebody's watching and waiting for him.
Yearning to hold him again to her heart;
There he lies—with the blue eyes dim,
And the smiling, child-like lips apart.
Tenderly bury the fair young dead.
Pausing to drop on his grave a tear;
Carve on the wooden slab at his head,
'Somebody's darling slumbers here!'"[450]

Mary Byson

"Red River Texas March 1864—Times are hard but I do not think we ought to complain. We have plenty of meat and bread and flour and sugar for the next year. I have been wearing homespun dresses this winter to save my calico and knit my stockings keeping my bought ones for summer. I am in hopes the war will end this year."[451]

Virginia McCollum Stinson

"On the morning of April 15th, 1864 all the women on West Washington Street and other streets in Camden who could were busy cooking rations for our dear men in grey. Everybody was excited for the news all day long was 'the Yankees are nearing town.' Women were flying about in the town to pay their last calls. They were not dressed in silk or fine hats or bonnets. There had been no 'Spring Opening' for three years. They wore sunbonnets or maybe nothing at all on their heads. I could not go out visiting on account of my feeble health, so my good neighbors came to see me. When the cry came 'the Yankees are in sight,' all the visitors rushed home and said good-bye. We did not know when we would meet again, for we women had resolved we would stay in our homes and save our household goods and stores."[452]

---

[450] Burton Egbert Stevenson, *The Home Book of Verse, American and English 1580-1918* (New York: Henry Holt & Company, 1918), 2318-2319.
[451] Katharine M. Jones, *Heroines Of Dixie Confederate: Women Tell Their Story Of The War* (New York: The Bobbs-Merrill Company, Inc., 1955), 275-276.
[452] Ibid., 278.

"Camden looked like a deserted town, no noise or Yankees in town, Oh! what a relief it was to be free of them. We did not know what joy was in store for us that day didn't know that our boys in grey were so near us, Oh! what joy when our dear men came marching in town what waving of hands and handkerchiefs, women and children greeting their loved ones. My husband came that night, my brother Hugh McCollum and Col. Grinstead came with their regiment at noon and so many of my dear soldier friends in grey came. All that day and night and the next day too they were coming. We did not have much to give them to eat, for the Yankees had almost robbed us of all we had of some things, but for all that we divided cheerfully with them, but they were hurrying on in pursuit of the Yankees, so their stay with us was brief."[453]

---

[453] Ibid., 284.

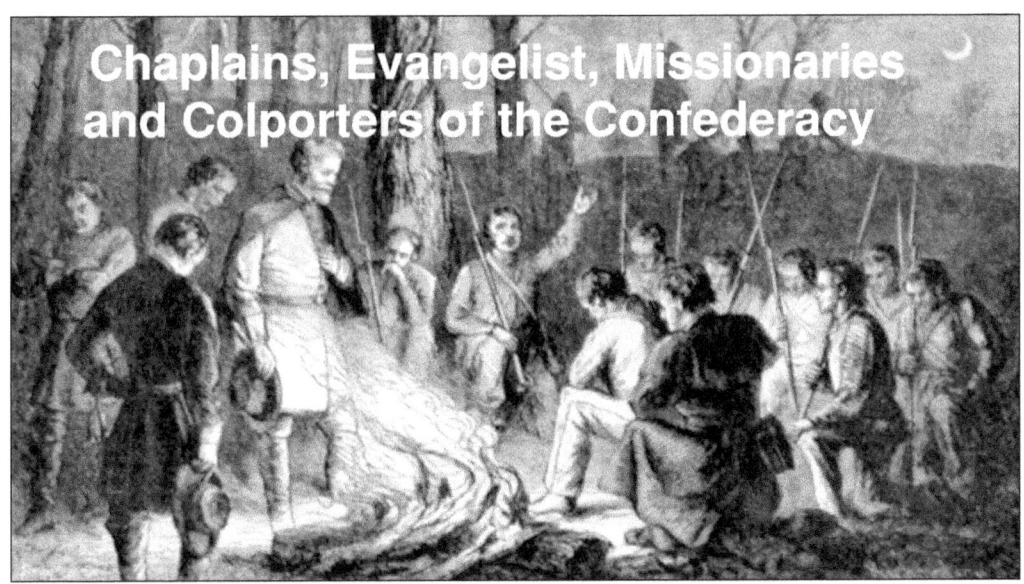

Chaplains, Evangelist, Missionaries and Colporters of the Confederacy

Beverly Tucker Lacy
W. B. Owen
J. C. Clopton
James Conway Hiden
T. J. McVeigh
A. L. Strough
J. M. B. Roach
J. E. Martin
J. H. Campbell
J. M. Carlisle
J. J. Hyman
J. M. Stokes
A. B. Campbell
S. W. Howerton
John H. Tomkies
J. J. D. Renfroe
William E. Wiatt
J. O. A. Cook
A. B. Woodfin
J. D. Leachman
J. W. Mills
J. C. Cranberry
Robert Ryland
M. D. Anderson

Hilary E. Hatcher
J. William Jones
Joseph C. Stiles
Joseph Cross
Isaac Taylor Tichnor
E. W. Yarbrough
Samuel S. Smith
E. J. Meynardie
W. C. Dunlap
William Hauser
P. A. Johnston
S. Strick
W. T. Bennett
W. H. Smith
Charles Todd Quintard
W. E. Jones
J. M. Cline
R. G. Porter
C. W. Miller
A. B. Stephens
Alexander Diego McVoy
Frederick Fitzgerald
Randolph H. McKim

"Oh, Thou God of the Universe ... we thank Thee for all the hallowed memories connected with our past history. Thou hast been the God of our fathers; oh, be Thou our God. Let it please Thee to vouchsafe Thy sacred presence to this assembly. ... We appeal to Thee, the searcher of hearts, for the purity and sincerity of our motives. If we are in violation of any compact still obligatory upon us with those States from which we have separated in order to set up a new government, ... we cannot hope for Thy presence and blessing. But oh, Thou heart-searching God, we trust that Thou seest we are pursuing those rights which were guaranteed to us by the solemn covenants of our fathers and which were cemented by their blood. And now we humbly recognize Thy hand in the Providence which has brought us together."[454]

Basil Manly

Beverly Tucker Lacy
Chaplain, Stonewall Jackson's Brigade

"I think it right that I should say to you, general, that the chaplains of this army have a deep interest in your welfare, and that some of the most fervent prayers we offer are in your behalf. The old hero's face flushed, tears started in his eyes, and he replied, with choked utterance and deep emotion: Please thank them for that, sir—I warmly appreciate it. And I can only say that I am nothing but a poor sinner, trusting in Christ alone for salvation, and need all of the prayers they can offer for me."[455]

---

[454] Felix Gregory de Fontaine, *History of American Abolitionism From 1787-1861: A Compendium of Historical Facts Embracing Legislation in Congress and Agitation Without* (New York: D. Appleton & Company, 1861), 59.

[455] J. William Jones, *Christ In the Camp or Religion in Lee's Army* (Richmond: B. F. Johnson, 1887), 50.

"There is a great harvest here, which ought to be reaped at once, and if it should pass this season we fear that much of it will be gathered by the enemy of souls."[456]

"'Oh, General! what a calamity!' Jackson thanked him with his usual courtesy, and added, with an unusual freedom: 'You see me severely wounded, but not depressed; not unhappy. I believe it has been done according to God's holy will, and I acquiesce entirely in it. You may think it strange, but you never saw me more perfectly contented than I am to-day; for I am sure that my Heavenly Father designs this affliction for my good. I am perfectly satisfied, that either in this life, or in that which is to come, I shall discover that what is now regarded as a calamity is a blessing. And if it appears a great calamity (as it surely will be a great inconvenience to be deprived of my arm), it will result in a great blessing. I can wait until God, in his own time, shall make known to me the object he has in thus afflicting me. But why should I not rather rejoice in it as a blessing, and not look on it as a calamity at all? If it were in my power to replace my arm, I would not dare to do it unless I could know it was the will of my Heavenly Father.'"[457]

W. B. Owen
Chaplain, Seventeenth Mississippi Regiment

"A package of tracts sent to Captain Ivey, Seventeenth Mississippi Regiment, came to hand, and I am glad of the opportunity to thank you for them, I assure you, had you been present as I passed up and down every company in our regiment distributing them, and seen how eagerly they were read by the soldiers, you would be stimulated to put forth every exertion to scatter such blessings continually among the soldiers. We have had considerable religious interest in our regiment; some have been converted, and others are seeking Jesus. If you can, do send us more tracts of different kinds, and 100 copies or more of that excellent tract, 'Come to Jesus.'"[458]

---

[456] Ibid., 340.

[457] William W. Bennett, *A Narrative of the Great Revival Which Prevailed in the Southern Armies During the Late Civil War* (Philadelphia: Claxton, Remsen, Haffelfinger, 1877), 295.

[458] J. William Jones, *Christ In the Camp or Religion in Lee's Army* (Richmond: B. F. Johnson, 1887), 175-176.

J. C. Clopton
Colporter

"*During my stay among the forces under General Jackson I heard little profanity. There are many pious. Christian men in this division of the army, and among others the general himself. I am told that he keeps on hand a supply of tracts, and occasionally goes among his men as a tract distributer. One of his aids inquired of me where tracts could be obtained, and gave me $5 to help on the cause.*"[459]

"*Passing along to the hospital and handing tracts to numbers of soldiers on the way, as I was approaching a man the evil one tempted me, suggesting that it was hardly worth while to give him one; but, going up to him and inquiring whether he was a Christian, I found instantly that he was under deep conviction of sin. 'Can you stop awhile with me? I wish to speak with you,' he said. Then, as we sat together, with tears and sobbings he told me of his sin-burdened heart, and asked to be directed to Jesus. Another, nigh unto death, said to me,' I am nearly to my journey's end, and, oh, sir, I would give worlds if I had them for the Christian's hope.' He seemed deeply moved, and I tried to explain to him the way. He has since passed to the spirit land.*"[460]

"*Oftentimes I see the soldiers reading the tracts for days after they have been received, and manifesting the most eager desire to be benefited by them. Passing along to the hospital, I saw a group of convalescents, and at once I was tempted to be ashamed of the work, and was about to pass them without giving any tracts; but it appeared to me that this might be a temptation of the evil one, and I determined to overlook no one. Going up to a soldier, I asked if he was a Christian. He was deeply moved, and replied, 'I wish to have some conversation with you; can you sit down with me awhile?' He told me that he had been a professor of religion; had enjoyed the smile of God on his soul; but that temptation and vice had led him astray, until now he was almost ready to despair. Weeping and sobbing he confessed his sin. I urged him to seek again the smile and favor of God. A very sick man said to me, 'Oh, sir, I would give worlds for an interest in salvation, and the pardon of sin.' He has since passed away.'*"[461]

---

[459] Ibid., 176.
[460] Ibid., 186.
[461] Ibid., 213-214.

James Conway Hiden
Chaplain, 60th Regiment, Virginia Infantry
(3rd Regiment, Wise Legion)

"I am holding a protracted meeting. Crowds attend the preaching, and some have professed a change of heart, while others are interested. It is an interesting sight to see men, wounded in every variety of way, sitting attentive to the story of the Cross."[462]

"In a stay of nearly a month, I have not heard three oaths, nor seen but one man under the influence of intoxicating liquor. We have preaching or prayer-meeting almost every day, and the attendance is large, and there is evidently considerable interest among the men. Many of them want Testaments and hymn-books, and eagerly seek after them, and all seem approachable on the subject of religion."[463]

"As I go along among the hospitals my heart is pained at seeing so much to be done and so few laborers. Sometimes I see several physicians going around together to consult about the physical man—to see if the body can be saved from the power of disease, while scarcely any one seems to be concerned about the disease of sin or the death which never dies. Every hospital ought to have at least one colporter. A poor, sick soldier, fifty-four years of age, was deeply affected by my visit to his couch and exclaimed, 'Thank God, a minister has come to pray with me.' Oh, I assure you, that to go to these sick men and to read to them the promises of the Gospel, and to invoke upon them the blessing of God, is the next thing to a visit of an angel. It relieves them from the sad gloom of the sick-room, and sends sunshine into their sorrowing hearts—the sunshine of heaven."[464]

"We heard a day or two since an incident related which we think should be published, as not only illustrating a fine trait of character in our young townsman, William M. Abell, who fell on the battle-field near Luray just a week ago, but as illustrating also the spirit of devotion to duty which actuates so widely all of our young men."[465]

---

[462] Ibid., 184.
[463] Ibid., 212.
[464] Ibid., 212-213.
[465] Ibid., 448.

T. J. McVeigh
Chaplain, Second Virginia Volunteers

"My supply of tracts has been distributed, and the soldiers ask for more. I administered the ordinance of baptism (for the first time) a few Sabbaths since, in the Appomattox river, to a young soldier from Alabama. It was the most deeply interesting and beautiful scene I ever witnessed. All of the soldiers who were able to leave their rooms gathered upon the banks of the river, and seemed to have a high appreciation of the ordinance."[466]

Albert L. Strough
Chaplain, Thirty-Seventh North Carolina Regiment

"In our retreat from Newberne, North Carolina, when overpowered by the superior force of the enemy, we lost nearly all the Testaments, etc., we had, and have not since been able to secure anything to read except fifteen small volumes presented to us by Kingston Baptist Church. Our regiment is now in four different directions, hence the chaplain cannot be with them all. Before we left North Carolina there were 137 in the regiment penitently inquiring after the Saviour."[467]

J. M. B. Roach
Chaplain, Tenth Alabama Regiment

"Just before the battle of Williamsburg, a lieutenant asked me for a copy of each of my tracts. He compressed them into as small a space as possible, and placed them in his pocket. During the battle he was struck by a ball which, in all probability, would have deprived him of life had it not lodged in the tracts, which were just over his heart. He seems solemnly affected, and I trust will soon be at the feet of Jesus."

---

[466] Ibid., 184.
[467] Ibid., 185.

J. E. Martin
Colporter

"One young man was very anxious to learn to read. I procured a spelling-book, and in a few days he learned so as to be able to read the Bible. He has since professed conversion."[468]

J. H. Campbell
Evangelist

"Noticing on the cars a soldier who looked sick and sad I offered him certain tracts which I hoped might suit his case. This led to a conversation, from which I learned that he had been dangerously ill in camp for many weeks, during which he had received intelligence of the death of his wife, who, he said, was 'one of the best women,' and that he was returning, broken in health, to his three little motherless children. But for the comforts of religion he thinks he would have lost his mind ; his fellow-soldiers came frequently into his tent, and read the Scriptures and sang and prayed with him."[469]

J. M. Carlisle
Chaplain, Seventh Regiment, South Carolina Volunteers

"As chaplain of the Seventh Regiment, South Carolina Volunteers, I desire to return thanks to certain unknown parties, in your city, for a donation of religious books and tracts forwarded to me for distribution among the soldiers. They were gladly received, and are being generally read, and I trust will be a positive good. May the blessing of God be upon those whose gift they are."[470]

"Our regiment is doing well. I try to preach on the Sabbath—usually twice. We have also a regimental prayer-meeting every evening at twilight. Upon these services there is usually a good attendance, and a serious attention that is very gratifying. Ask for us the prayers of all."[471]

---

[468] Ibid., 217.
[469] Ibid., 217-218.
[470] Ibid., 267.
[471] William W. Bennett, *A Narrative of the Great Revival Which Prevailed in the Southern Armies During the Late Civil War* (Philadelphia: Claxton, Remsen,

J. J. Hyman
Chaplain, Forty-Ninth Georgia Regiment

"On the following Monday night, after all became quiet, I opened a meeting, as usual, in one of the companies, to have what we call family prayer before retiring to rest. Seeing so many making their way towards where we were singing, after singing one hymn we called on one brother, and then another, to lead in prayer. We had what might be called an old-fashioned prayer meeting, with about six hundred soldiers present. After several prayers had been offered, for a few moments all was silent. I must say, I never had such feelings before; such crying I never heard—not aloud, but with deep sobbing. The stoutest and hardest hearts were softened—not a word of exhortation was given—all was the effect of singing and prayer. I gave an invitation to anxious ones to come forward for prayer, and probably 300 responded."[472]

J. M. Stokes
Chaplain, Wright's Georgia Brigade

"I am happy to state that the health of our troops seems to be much better than it was a few months since. It will be a source of delight to Christians and all thinking people to know that the religious element among our troops is much greater now than at any time previous since the war began. I believe sincerely that there is less profanity in a week now, than there was in a day six months ago. And I am quite sure there are ten who attend religious services now to one who attended six months ago, I speak principally with reference to our own regiment, but I have been informed by those who have travelled among the different parts of the army in Virginia that such is the case everywhere."[473]

"Zion is flourishing again in this army. There are as many as twenty chapels. We have had a meeting in progress two weeks, and the interest is increasing daily. We have had several conversions, and there were, I reckon, fifty

---

Haffelfinger, 1877), 54.

[472] J. William Jones, *Christ In the Camp or Religion in Lee's Army* (Richmond: B. F. Johnson, 1887), 279-280.

[473] William W. Bennett, *A Narrative of the Great Revival Which Prevailed in the Southern Armies During the Late Civil War* (Philadelphia: Claxton, Remsen, Haffelfinger, 1877), 176.

mourners at the altar for prayer last evening. Our chapel seats between 300 and 400, and is full every night unless the weather is very inclement."[474]

A. B. Campbell
Chaplain, Ninth Georgia Regiment

"From the time we left the Peninsula until now, we have never suffered an opportunity to hold meetings to pass unimproved. Many souls have been converted, and Christians in the army have been greatly revived, and many who had fearfully backslidden have been reclaimed. Two of these young men have fallen in battle. As one of them fell at Manassas, he turned his dying eyes to his companions, and said: 'Write to mother, and tell all the family to meet me in heaven, for I am going there.' The other was wounded there also, and subsequently died—declaring to the last that he was 'willing to depart and be with Christ.' Others of the young converts are with us, battling nobly for the cause of Christ. It is no longer a question whether the work of God can be carried on in an army."[475]

S. W. Howerton
Chaplain, Fifteenth North Carolina Regiment

"Every company has prayers, nightly, immediately after roll-call, and nearly all attend and are respectful; the officers, in some instances, conducting the exercises and leading in prayer."[476]

John H. Tomkies
Chaplain, Seventh Florida Regiment

"On last evening fifteen were buried with Christ in baptism. And still the good work goes on. Our meetings are increasing in interest, and each evening scores of soldiers are inquiring, 'What shall we do to be saved?' Brother Kitzmiller has been laboring with us with a zeal and earnestness characteristic of a true Christian."[477]

---

[474] Ibid., 361.
[475] J. William Jones, *Christ In the Camp or Religion in Lee's Army* (Richmond: B. F. Johnson, 1887), 294-295.
[476] Ibid., 316.
[477] Ibid., 322.

J. J. D. Renfroe
Chaplain, Tenth Alabama Regiment

"We have a splendid protracted meeting in progress in the brigade. About twenty-five have been baptized, and others have joined other Churches and the interest is increasing. I believe that 100 anxious souls presented themselves for prayer last night after the sermon."[478]

"I have never seen such a time before or since. There were as many evidences of genuine penitence as I ever noted at home-yes more. Almost every day there would be a dozen conversions, and there were in the six weeks in the brigade, not less than five hundred who professed conversion. Not all of our brigade, for there was a battalion of artillery camped near us, and other brigades, who attended our preaching, many of whom professed religion. We estimated the conversions then at five hundred and fifty."[479]

William E. Wiatt
Chaplain, Twenty-Sixth Virginia Regiment

"We have been holding prayer-meetings constantly in the chapel for weeks, and we scarcely ever fail, how tired soever the men may be,, to have a large congregation. It is a glorious sight to behold a hundred or two of young Christians mingling their voices in praise to their Saviour. Many of them exhort and pray in public, and there is quite a development of piety and of gifts. We have inquirers still, and some are giving their hearts to the Saviour."[480]

"It gives me great pleasure to inform you and the friends of our regiment, through the Herald, that the Lord continues to pour out His Spirit upon us. During the three months and a half of our camping here, about twenty-five of our officers and men have professed Christ. I have already baptized fifteen, and several more will follow. Conversions are reported almost every week. Prayer-meetings are held in all of the companies nightly, except when some providential circumstance prevents. A great deal of zeal and love for Christ are exhibited by both old and young professors. We have a flourishing

---

[478] Ibid., 324.
[479] Ibid., 511.
[480] Ibid., 331.

Christian Association, composed of some two hundred or more members, whose stated meetings are once in two weeks."[481]

J. O. A. Cook
Chaplain, Second Georgia Battalion, Wright's Brigade

"It would do your heart good to witness our camp-services, to see the immense throngs that crowd our rude chapels, to listen to the soul-stirring music, as with one voice and one heart they unite in singing the sweet songs of Zion, and to note the deep interest and solemn earnestness with which they listen to the preaching of the word. I have never seen anything like it. I can but believe that the blessing of God is upon us, and that He is preparing us for a speedy and glorious peace."[482]

A. B. Woodfin
Chaplain, Sixty-First Georgia Regiment

"The Lord is with us. For about two weeks past we have been rejoicing in His presence and His blessing. There is a deep religious interest pervading this whole brigade. Scores are nightly inquiring the way of life, and a goodly number profess to have found it. It was my happy privilege on . yesterday, in the presence of a large congregation, 'to bury' sixteen 'by baptism.' Oh, may this interest not subside while the war lasts—nay, may it continue even when it shall have closed; and may these Christ loving soldiers go home to be as holy firebrands in our Churches!"[483]

"Our nightly meetings are still kept up, with most encouraging results. Almost every day witnesses the joyful conversion of some precious souls, and many are still anxiously asking, 'What must I do to be saved?' Since our meeting commenced we have baptized fifty, and on tomorrow we expect to baptize about ten others. About one hundred of the brigade have professed faith in Christ. We would render all the praise unto Him to whom belongeth salvation."[484]

---

[481] Ibid., 357.
[482] Ibid., 340.
[483] Ibid., 371.
[484] Ibid., 374.

J. D. Leachman
Chaplain, Twentieth Virginia Regiment Cavalry

"The chaplains of this (Colonel Jackson's) brigade have recently closed a very interesting meeting of nineteen days. There were twenty-five or thirty conversions. I baptized nine, and five others are received for baptism. Seven united with the Southern Methodists. Many penitents are inquiring the way of salvation. We hope the good work thus commenced will continue. We had the assistance of several ministers at different times during the meeting."[485]

J. W. Mills
Chaplain

"Many of our regiment fell in the terrible battle of Sharpsburg. We occupied the centre, where the enemy made his fiercest attack, hoping to break our lines in that vital part of the field, and so win the day. The enemy were formed in a semicircle on the side of a hill. Our brave men marched up to the attack until they could see the heads and shoulders of their adversaries over the summit of the hill, when firing commenced. From the two wings and the centre of this semicircle they poured upon us a murderous fire for about one hour. Five times our colors fell, but as often our men rushed to the spot and raised them to the breeze."[486]

J. C. Cranberry
Chaplain, Eleventh Virginia Regiment

"I shall never cease to remember with admiration one of the earliest victims of this war. Major Carter Harrison, of the Eleventh Virginia. He was an earnest servant of Christ; modest, firm, unostentatious, zealous. He seized at once the hearts of the regiment by his many virtues, by his courtesy to all and his kind visits to the sick, to whom he bore a word not only of sympathy, but also of pious exhortation."[487]

---

[485] Ibid., 371-372.
[486] Ibid., 409.
[487] Ibid., 405-406.

Robert Ryland
Colporter

"I have, from almost the beginning of the war, been laboring as colporter in the hospitals of Richmond, and my impression is that the results of this work are infinitely greater and more glorious than many believe. As to myself, every week's observation would have enabled me to write out facts and incidents of the most cheering character, enough to fill up half of the Religious Herald, and yet I have written but a few lines, leaving unpublished this great mass of facts, illustrative of the good this work is doing."[488]

M. D. Anderson
Colporter

"A glorious revival is going on in Major Henry's Battalion, Captain Riley's Battery. I have been laboring with them several days, meeting twice a day. The men are deeply interested in the meetings. Four have professed a hope in Christ and many are seriously concerned. Last night twelve came forward for prayer. Dr. W. F. Broaddus has promised to preach for us tonight. Will not some of our brethren come and assist us in this glorious work? The brethren in the company take a lively interest in it. I have been distributing a great many copies of the Herald among them, and find they are eagerly sought after. Pray for us, dear brethren, that this work may continue until all of this company shall become faithful and happy Christians."[489]

Hilary E. Hatcher
Chaplain, Malone's Brigade

"It gives me pleasure to report more definitely this week, the state of religious interest in Mahone's Brigade, where we have been holding a series of meetings for three weeks. On last Sabbath, Brother Andrew Broaddus, Jr., at my request, baptized thirty-one candidates for admission into the Baptist Church; nineteen others are awaiting to be baptized, and I learn that others will report themselves in a few days. At present 146 are reported to have found peace in Christ, and have asked for membership among some one of

---

[488] Ibid., 181.
[489] Ibid., 324.

the evangelical denominations. The interest is unabated. Scores and hundreds are asking, 'What must we do to be saved?'[490]

J. William Jones
Chaplain, Thirteenth Virginia Regiment

"March 3, 1864—Now is the time to preach in the army. There is a half formed intention on the part of many of our brethren that they will come to the army when the weather opens, and spend a while in preaching to the soldiers. Let me urge that they come at once. There are comfortable houses of worship (thirty-seven in all) scattered throughout our camps ; there is a good prospect of weeks of uninterrupted labor, and there is an eagerness to hear the Gospel seldom witnessed in camp. Many of our chaplains are now absent, taking a needed respite from their labors, and there are now comparatively few missionaries in the camps; so that, at a time when there is special demand for ministerial labors, the supply is unusually limited. I appeal, then, to our brethren in the ministry (especially to our most useful pastors) to come at once, if only for a short time, and give us a helping hand in reaping the precious sheaves now 'white unto the harvest.' It will cost some trouble and sacrifice—but ought we not to be willing to endure these for the good of the noble fellows who risk their all for us? And do not delay your coming, brethren, for there is many a poor fellow whom you might reach now, who will fill a soldier's grave in the early spring campaign. Take your roll of blankets and a box of provisions (if convenient) to help the 'mess' with which you may stay, and come right along."[491]

Joseph C. Stiles
Missionary

"So deep and enduring was the religious interest awakened by the Fredericksburg revival, that in an artillery company two souls, probably made anxious by the zealous piety of a comrade who had enjoyed himself abundantly at the Fredericksburg meeting, were converted in the midst of the severest fighting in the late battle while others felt that they were almost in heaven, and could hardly suppress their exultant religious shouts amid the

---
[490] Ibid., 330.
[491] Ibid., 367.

loudest roar and din of the conflict, the slaughter of the cannoneers of their own guns, and the palpable peril of their own lives."[492]

"They form camp churches of all the Christians of every denomination in their regiments. The members are expected to practice all the duties of brotherly love, Christian watchfulness, and Christian discipline. Indeed, they are taught to feel themselves under every obligation of strict membership. The chaplain writes to every minister or church, with which the member may have been connected, or the young convert desires to be united, and, giving the name of the person, solicits the prayers of the said church, both for the individual and the whole camp church, and by correspondence keeps them apprised of the walk and history of the party."[493]

Joseph Cross
Chaplain, General Bragg's Army

"It is interesting to see how they flock to our nightly prayer-meetings, frequently in greater numbers than your Sabbath congregations in some of your city churches. I preach to them twice on the Lord's day, seated around me on the ground, officers and men, in the most primitive order you can imagine. But the most interesting, probably the most useful, part of my work is the visitation of the sick. Every morning I go to the hospital, visiting the several apartments successively; in each of which I talk privately with the men, then read a passage of Holy Scripture, make some remarks upon it, and finish with prayer. However wicked and thoughtless the}^ are in camp, they are all glad to see the chaplain when they are sick; and I have yet to meet with the first instance of any other than the most respectful and reverent attention. I think I never occupied a field that afforded an equal opportunity for usefulness."[494]

---

[492] Ibid., 301-302

[493] William W. Bennett, *A Narrative of the Great Revival Which Prevailed in the Southern Armies During the Late Civil War* (Philadelphia: Claxton, Remsen, Haffelfinger, 1877), 54.

[494] William W. Bennett, *A Narrative of the Great Revival Which Prevailed in the Southern Armies During the Late Civil War* (Philadelphia: Claxton, Remsen, Haffelfinger, 1877), 120.

Isaac Taylor Tichnor
Chaplain, Seventeenth Alabama Regiment

"During this engagement we were under a cross fire on the left wing from three directions. Under it the boys wavered. I had been wearied, and was sitting down, but seeing them waver, I sprang to my feet, took off my hat, waved it over my head, walked up and down the line, and, as they say, 'preached them a sermon.' I reminded them that it was Sunday. That at that hour (11:30 o'clock) all their home folks were praying for them, that Tom Watts (excuse the familiar way in which I employed so distinguished a name) had told us he would listen with an eager ear to hear from the 17th; and shouting your name loud over the roar of battle, I called upon them to stand there and die, if need be, for their country. The effect was evident. Every man stood to his post, every eye flashed, and every heart beat high with desperate resolve to conquer or die. The regiment lost one-third of the number carried into the field."[495]

E. W. Yarbrough
Chaplain

"Before leaving, Colonel Zachry proposed to show me 'Stonewall Jackson,' if I would ride with him a short distance. We found him quartered under an apple tree, and at work of course. My first impressions of this Southern Boanerges will never be forgotten. His form is slender, not very erect, and of medium height. His lion heart is concealed under as pleasant a countenance as I ever saw. Had we met on the road before this war broke out, I would have taken him for a Methodist itinerant preacher on his way to an appointment pondering a most serious discourse. Notwithstanding all the feebleness of form and sweetness of expression, he was the hero of the Valley, having clipped the wings of at least four soaring Federal Generals in a short time, and having thundered upon McClellan's rear simultaneously with the advance of our forces upon his front, completely unearthing him, and then joining with his shouting hosts in the most glorious pursuit of an invading foe ever recorded."[496]

---

[495] J. William Jones, *Christ In the Camp or Religion in Lee's Army* (Richmond: B. F. Johnson, 1887), 147.

[496] William W. Bennett, *A Narrative of the Great Revival Which Prevailed in the Southern Armies During the Late Civil War* (Philadelphia: Claxton, Remsen, Haffelfinger, 1877), 160.

Samuel S. Smith
Chaplain, Sixtieth Georgia Regiment

"About the first and middle of October, we held a series of meetings in camps, during which time many souls were renewed and encouraged, several were made happy in the love of God, and the altar was crowded from day to day with seekers of religion. The like was hardly ever before witnessed in camps."[497]

E. J. Meynardie
Chaplain, Keitts' Regiment of South Carolina Volunteers

"On Thursday evening, 25th ult., the religious interest, which for some time had been quite apparent, became so deep and manifest that I determined to hold a series of meetings, during which, up to last night, ninety-three applied for membership in the various branches of the Church, nearly all of whom profess conversion. Every night the church at which we worship was densely crowded, and obvious seriousness pervaded the congregation. To the invitation to approach the altar for prayer prompt and anxious responses were made; and it was indeed an unusual and impressive spectacle to behold the soldiers of the country, ready for battle, and even for death on the battle-field, bowed in prayer for that blessing which the warrior, of all others, so much needs. God was with us most graciously, and it was a period of profound interest and great joy."[498]

W. C. Dunlap
Chaplain, Eighth Georgia Regiment

"God has wonderfully blessed us of late. We have had going on in our midst a revival of religion, with more or less interest, since the battles in front of Richmond. Recently, however, it has grown greatly in interest; and before breaking up camps near Fredericksburg, the Lord was doing a mighty work in our midst."[499]

---

[497] Ibid., 209.
[498] J. William Jones, *Christ In the Camp or Religion in Lee's Army* (Richmond: B. F. Johnson, 1887), 211.
[499] William W. Bennett, *A Narrative of the Great Revival Which Prevailed in the Southern Armies During the Late Civil War* (Philadelphia: Claxton, Remsen, Haffelfinger, 1877), 254.

William Hauser
Chaplain, Forty-Eighth Georgia Regiment

"The precious leaves from the tree of life are healing our sin-diseased soldiers. Swearing, and all other crimes incident to an army, are evidently diminishing, and deep piety is on the increase. Every night the holy songs of Zion go up on this balmy spring air, a sweet incense, I think, to the throne of the Eternal. Prayer-meetings are held every night in several of our companies, and a great desire is manifested to get Hymn-Books. Bless the Lord! He is working among us, and giving us, I do not doubt, a silent yet precious revival of religion, the effects of which are seen more and more plainly every day. It would do you some good to see how eagerly these gallant, weather-beaten warriors crowd around me to get tracts every time I have a new supply; but they want and much need something fresh every Sunday to engage their minds and keep them from resorting to ball-plays and cards. Our Colonel is not religious, but he has the greatest respect for Christianity, and seems to take great delight in affording me every facility for my work."[500]

P. A. Johnston
Chaplain, 38th Mississippi Volunteers

"The Lord is at work among us. His stately steppings are often heard and his presence felt to the comfort of our souls. We have had for the past week very interesting prayer-meetings. They were well-attended and the very highest interest manifested. Souls are hungry for the 'bread of life.'"[501]

S. Strick
Chaplain, Fifty-Ninth Tennessee Regiment

"God is at work among our men. Many are earnestly seeking the pardon of their sins—some have been converted. Our nightly prayer-meetings are well-attended by anxious listeners, and my tent is crowded daily by deeply penitent souls. Never have I known such a state of religious feeling in our army as at this time. God's Spirit is moving the hearts of our soldiers."[502]

---

[500] Ibid., 262-263.
[501] Ibid., 268.
[502] Ibid., 274.

W. T. Bennett
Chaplain, Twelfth Tennessee Regiment, Polk's Corps

"Our regiment is being greatly blessed. We meet from night to night for exhortation, instruction, and prayer. Already, there have been upwards of thirty conversions. Most of them have joined the Church. There are yet a large number of inquirers. The moral tone of the regiment seems rapidly changing for the better."[503]

W. H. Smith
Chaplain

"Brethren! ministers! are you asleep? Do you not hear the cries of our countrymen calling to you from every part of the land? The soldiers feel their need of salvation, and are crying for the gospel! And will you withhold it from them? Awake! arise! gird yourselves with the whole armor of God, and come forth 'to the help of the Lord, to the help of the Lord against the mighty.'"[504]

Charles Todd Quintard
Chaplain, Twelfth Tennessee Regiment, Polk's Corps

"We feel that we need only mention the fact that our brave soldiers are asking for the Word of Life in order to secure from a generous public the most liberal contributions. Who can withhold, when the sick and wounded who fill our hospitals ask for the word of God to cheer and sustain them during their days of affliction, their nights of weariness and suffering? We feel confident that there are many who will give neither grudgingly nor of necessity, but with cheerful hearts and liberal hands. The religious interests of our soldiers demand and must receive prompt attention from every lover of good order, civil liberty, and piety towards God."[505]

---

[503] Ibid., 276.
[504] Ibid., 276.
[505] Ibid., 277.

W. E. Jones
Chaplain, Twenty-Second Georgia Regiment

"The Lord is in our midst. Ever since the last great victory God has been pouring out upon this regiment his Spirit, almost without measure, and many have been converted, and forty-five have joined different branches of the Church, and there is a host of mourning souls. They rush to the altar by scores. The work is prospering throughout our entire army. I earnestly call upon all God's people, and especially upon parents, wives, and sisters, to pray for the salvation of these precious souls."[506]

J. M. Cline
Chaplain, Fifty-Second North Carolina Regiment

"God has blessed our regiment with a most glorious revival of religion. God has indeed been with us. During the last ten days fifty-six have joined the Church, and thirty-three have been soundly converted. The Lord has done great things for us. Lions have been changed to lambs. I never witnessed such a glorious revival before. The Church is greatly revived, and built up in the most holy faith. On last Sabbath I administered the sacrament of the Lord's Supper to one hundred and fifteen communicants. God was with us, and we had a refreshing season from the presence of the Lord. The revival is still progressing."[507]

R. G. Porter
Chaplain, Tenth Mississippi Regiment

"It makes my very soul happy to witness the manifestations of God's saving power as seen here in the army—from ten to forty at the altar of prayer—have preaching every day when not hindered by the men being called off."[508]

---

[506] Ibid., 308.
[507] Ibid., 309.
[508] Ibid., 314.

C. W. Miller
Missionary, D. H. Hill's Corps

"Since I arrived here as missionary I have been engaged every night in religious services with the soldiers. A revival and extensive awakening have been in progress in General Bate's brigade for four weeks. Every night the altar is crowded with weeping penitents. Several have been happily converted. To me it is the most interesting sight of my life. You cannot look upon these penitent, weeping men at the altar of prayer without thinking of the bloody fields of Perryville and Murfreesboro, and the victorious veterans rolling up to heaven the shouts of triumph. Here they are. Some sending up the note of a more glorious victory—others charging through the columns of the foe to 'take the kingdom of heaven by force.'"[509]

A. B. Stephens
Chaplain, Eleventh South Carolina Regiment

"We now constitute the garrison at Fort Sumter. On the last fast-day I began a meeting which has been going on and increasing in interest all the while till now. God has honored us with a gracious revival of religion among the soldiery of this command. A few months ago but two officers in the regiment were members of the Church. Now but few more than that number are not professors of religion. About 200 have joined the Church, and a larger number have been converted and are now happy in the love of God. It would do your soul good to visit the old Fort, battered and scarred as it is, and hear the soldiers make the battered walls ring with the high praises of the living God. No camp-meeting that I have ever attended can come near it."[510]

Alexander Diego McVoy
Chaplain, Thirty-eighth Alabama Regiment

"I witnessed the passing away of a Louisianian of Gibson's brigade, 4th La., the other day. Seldom have I seen a stronger Christian faith, a firmer reliance on God, and a clearer assurance of salvation in a dying hour. He

---

[509] Ibid., 314.
[510] Ibid., 330.

was cruelly lacerated by a piece of shell that had ploughed deeply across his right side, aud his sufferings were intense and unremitted. Still his mind was fixed upon God."[511]

Frederick Fitzgerald
Chaplain

"I have perceived a constant and real improvement in the moral and religious character of our soldiers since the first nine months of the war. I believe that there is far less of vice of every kind in our army than there was one year ago, and far more seriousness and willingness to read God's Word and hear it explained; far more interest in things that pertain to the soul, about that world where peace reigns eternal, and the horrid sound of war is never heard."[512]

Randolph H. McKim
Chaplain, Second Virginia Cavalry

"As a chaplain on the firing line with the men, I had nothing to do but to sit on my horse and be shot at (unarmed, of course), waiting for a call to attend some wounded man. Having passed through both experiences, I can say that the role of a chaplain at the fiery front takes more nerve 'by a jugful' than that of a staff officer. Yet I am certain that the chaplain who sticks to his men through thick and thin will have tenfold influence over them for that reason."[513]

"We must forevermore do honor to our heroic dead. We must forevermore cherish the sacred memories of those four terrible but glorious years of unequal strife. We must forevermore consecrate in our hearts our old battle flag of the Southern Cross – not now as a political symbol, but as the consecrated emblem of an heroic epoch. The people that forgets its heroic dead

---

[511] Ibid., 396-397.
[512] Joseph Blount Cheshire, *The Church in the Confederate States* (Longman, Green & Company, 1912), 73.
[513] Randolph H. McKim, *Chaplain, A Soldier's Recollections: Leaves From the Diary of a Young Confederate* (Longmans, Green & Company, 1910), 226.

is already dying at the heart, and we believe we shall be truer and better citizens of the United States if we are true to our past."[514]

"I do not believe the valor and devotion of the armies of the South were so lavishly poured out in vain. By their all-sacrificing patriotism they arraigned before the world the usurpation of powers and functions which by the Constitution were reserved to the States — and their arraignment has not been in vain."[515]

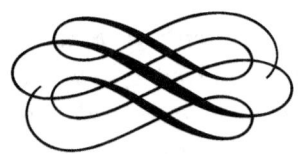

---

[514] Randolph H. McKim, *Chaplain, A Soldier's Recollections: Leaves From the Diary of a Young Confederate* (Longmans, Green & Company, 1910), 279.
[515] Randolph H. McKim, *Chaplain, A Soldier's Recollections: Leaves From the Diary of a Young Confederate* (Longmans, Green & Company, 1910), 280.

Bibliography

A Memorial of the Hon. George Davis (Wilmington, N.C., Chamber of Commerce,1896).

A Review of the First Volume of Alexander H. Stephens's War Between the States By Constitutionalist (Philadelphia: J. P. Lippincott & Company, 1872).

Co. Aytch, Maury Grays, First Tennessee Regiment; or A Side Show of the Big Show (Chattanooga, Tennessee: Times Printing Company, 1900).

Harper's New Monthly Magazine, Volume 98, Dec 1898-May 1889 (New York: Harper & Brothers, Publishers, 1899).

Inaugural Address of Gov. Thomas H. Watts Before the Alabama Legislature, December 1, 1863 (Montgomery: Montgomery Advertiser Book and Job Offices, 1863).

Lee Considered: General Robert E. Lee and Civil War History (UNC Press Books, 1996).

P. G. T. Beauregard, A Proclamation. To the Good People of the Counties of Alexandria, Loudoun, Fairfax, and Prince William (June 5, 1861, Alexandria, Virginia).

Reminiscences of the Women of Missouri During the Sixties (Missouri Division, United Daughters of the Confederacy: 1920).

Report of the Proceedings of the Reunions of the Society of the Army of the Tennessee, Volume 33 (Society of the Army of the Tennessee, 1902).

South Carolina Women in the Confederacy, Volume 2 (Columbia, S. C.: The State Company, 1907).

Speech of Hon. Gustavus A. Henry of Tennessee, in the Senate of the Confederate States (November 29, 1864).

Speech of Hon. J. P. Benjamin, of Louisiana, on the right of secession delivered in the Senate of the United States (December 31, 1860).

Speech of Hon. R. M. T. Hunter, of Virginia, On the Resolution Proposing to Retrocede the Forts, Dock-Yards, to the States Applying For the Same (January 11, 1861).

Speech of Hon. Robert Toombs: On the Crisis. Delivered Before the Georgia Legislature, December 7, 1860 (Lemuel Towers, 1860).

Speech of Hon. W. S. Oldham, of Texas on the resolutions of the State of Texas, concerning peace, reconstruction and independence. In the Confederate States Senate (January 30, 1865).

Speeches of Willam L. Yancey, Esq., Senator From the State of Alabama Made in the Senate of the Confederate States During the Session Commencing On the 18th day of August, A.D. 1862 (Montgomery Advertiser Book and Job Office, 1862).

State of the Country, Speech of Hon. A. G. Brown of Mississippi, In the Confederate Senate (December 24, 1863).

The Chautauquan, Volume 30 (Chautauqua Press, 1900).

The Heart of a Soldier as Revealed in the Intimate Letters of Genl. George E. Pickett, CSA (New York: Seth Moyle, 1913).

Addey, Markinfield, *Life and Imprisonment of Jefferson Davis, Together With the Life and Military Career of Stonewall Jackson* (New York: M. Doolady, Publisher, 1866).

Alfriend, Frank H., *The Life of Jefferson Davis* (Cincinnati: National Publishing House, 1868).

Allan, Francis D., *Allan's Lone Star Ballads: A Collection of Southern Patriotic Songs, Made During Confederate Times* (Galveston: J. D. Sawyer Publisher, 1874).

Allan, William, *History of the Campaign of Gen. T.J. (Stonewall) Jackson in the Shenandoah Valley of Virginia* (Philadelphia: J. B. Lippincott & Company, 1880).

Allan, William, *Stonewall Jackson, Robert E. Lee, and the Army of Northern Virginia*, 1862 (Da Capo Press, 1880).

Alexander, Edward Porter, *Military Memoirs of A Confederate: A Critical Narrative* (New York: Scribner's Sons, 1907).

Allsopp, Fred W., *The Life Story of Albert Pike* (Parke-Harper, Audigier & Price, 1920).

Andrews, Eliza Frances, *The War-Time Journal of a Georgia Girl, 1864-1865* (D. Appleton & Company, 1808).

Arnold, Thomas Jackson, *Early Life and Letters of General Thomas J. Jackson: "Stonewall" Jackson* (Fleming H. Revell Company, 1916).

Avary, Myrta Lockett, *Recollections of Alexander H. Stephens* (New York: Doubleday, Page & Company, 1910).

Basler, Roy P., *The Collected Works of Abraham Lincoln*, Volume 1 (Rutgers University Press, New Brunswich, New Jersey, 1953).

Bennett, William J., *America: The Last Best Hope* Volumes I and II (Thomas Nelson Inc, 2007).

Bennett, William W., *A Narrative of the Great Revival Which Prevailed in the Southern Armies During the Late Civil War* (Philadelphia: Claxton, Remsen, Haffelfinger, 1877).

Berry, Thomas F., *Four Years With Morgan and Forrest* (Harlow-Ratllff Company, 1914).

Boyd, Belle, *Belle Boyd In Camp and Prison*, Vol. 1 (London: Saunders, Otley and Company, 1865).

Boyd, Belle, *Belle Boyd In Camp and Prison*, Vol. 2 (London: Saunders, Otley and Company, 1865).

Blackford, W. W., *War Years With JEB Stuart* (New York: Charles Scribner's Sons, 1946).

Bradford, Gamaliel, *Confederate Portraits* (Houghton Mifflin Company, 1914).

Brock, R. A., *Southern Historical Society Papers*, Volume 17 (Richmond: Published by the Society, 1876).

Bruce, Philip Alexander, *Robert E. Lee* (G.W. Jacobs, 1907).

Buck, Irving A., *Cleburne and His Command* (New York, The Neale Publishing Company, 1908).

Butler, Pierce, *Judah P. Benjamin* (Philadelphia: George W. Jacobs & Company Publishers, 1906).

Capers, Henry D., *The life and Times of Christopher Gustavus Memminger* (Richmond: Everett Waddey Company, Publishers.1893).

Chase, William C., *Story of Stonewall Jackson: A Narrative of the Career of Thomas Jonathan (Stonewall) Jackson, from Written and Verbal Accounts of His Life* (D. E. Luther Publishing Company, 1901).

Cheshire, Joseph Blount, *The Church in the Confederate States* (Longman, Green & Company, 1912).

Chesnut, Mary Boykin, *A Diary From Dixie* (New York: D. Appleton & Company, 1906).

Christy, Robert, *Proverbs, Maxims and Phrases of All Ages*, Volume 1 (New York: C. P. Putnam's Sons, 1888).

Cisco, Walter Brian, *Wade Hampton, Confederate Warrior, Conservative Statesman* (Potomac Books, Inc., 2004).

Cleveland, Henry, *Alexander H. Stephens in Public and Private With Letters and Speeches, Before, During, and Since the War* (National Publishing Company, 1886).

Cooke, John Esten, Hoge, Moses Drury, Jones, John William, *Stonewall Jackson: A Military Biography* (New York: A. Appleton and Company, 1876).

Crocker, H. W., *Robert E. Lee on Leadership: Executive Lessons in Character, Courage, and Vision* (Random House, 2010).

Crocker, H. W., *The Politically Incorrect Guide to the Civil War* (Regnery Publishing, 2008).

Cutrer, Thomas W., Parrish, T. Michael, *Brothers in Gray: The Civil War Letters of the Pierson Family* (LSU Press, 2004).

Cutting, Elisabeth, *Jefferson Davis: Political Soldier* (New York: Dodd, Mead & Company, 1930).

Dabney, Robert Lewis, *Life and Campaigns of Lieut.-Gen. Thomas J. Jackson* (Blelock & Company, 1866).

Davis, Donald A., *Stonewall Jackson* (Palgrave Macmillan, 2007).

Davis, Jefferson, *The Rise and Fall of the Confederate Government*, Volume 1 (New York: A. Appleton & Company, 1881).

Davis, Nicholas A., *The Campaign From Texas to Maryland With the Battle of Fredericksburg* (Richmond: Presbyterian Committee of Publication of the Confederate States, 1863).

Davis, Varina, *Jefferson Davis: Ex-President of the Confederate States of America*, Volume 2 (New York: Belford Company, Publishers, 1890).

Dawson, Sarah Morgan, *A Confederate Girl's Diary* (New York: Houghton Mifflin Company, 1913).

de Fontaine, Felix Gregory, *History of American Abolitionism From 1787-1861: A Compendium of Historical Facts Embracing Legislation in Congress and Agitation Without* (New York: D. Appleton & Company, 1861).

Delaune, Lena Young De Grumond, *JEB Stuart* (Pelican Publishing, 1962).

Dedmondt, Glenn, *The Flags of Civil War Arkansas* (Pelican Publishing, 2009).

DeRosa, Marshall L., *The Enduring Relevance of Robert E. Lee: The Ideological Warfare Underpinning the American Civil War* (Lexington Books, 2013).

Dodd, William E., *Jefferson Davis* (Philadelphia: George W. Jacobs & Company, 1907).

DuBose, John Witherspoon, *General Joseph Wheeler And Army Of Tennessee* (New York: The Neale Publishing Company, 1912).

Earnest, Joseph Brummell, *The Religious Development of the Negro in Virginia* (Charlottesville, Virginia: The Michie Company, Printers, 1914).

Elder, Susan Blanchard, *The Confederate Flag* (Blackmar & Brothers, 1861).

Fellman, Michael, *The Making of Robert E. Lee* (JHU Press, 2003).

Flood, Theodore L. and Bray, Frank Chapin, *The Chautauquan*, Volume 31 (1900).

Foote, Shelby, *The Civil War: A Narrative: Volume 1: Fort Sumter to Perryville* (New York: Random House, 1958).

Freeman, Douglas Southall, *Lee's Lieutenants: Cedar Mountain to Chancellorsville* (Simon and Schuster, 1997).

Gay, Mary Ann Harris, *Life in Dixie During the War 1863-1864-1865* (Atlanta: Constitutional Job Office, 1892).

Greenhow, Rose, *My Imprisonment and the First Year of Abolition Rule at Washington* (London: Richard Bentley, Publisher in Ordinary to Her Majesty, 1863).

Grissom, Michael Andrew, *Southern by the Grace of God* (Pelican Publishing, 1989).

Hamilton, J. G. DeRoulhac and Hamilton, Mary Thompson, *The Life of Robert E. Lee for Boys and Girls* (Houghton Mifflin Company, 1917).

Hartje, Robert George, *Van Dorn: The Life and Times of a Confederate General* (Vanderbilt University Press, 1967).

Herrera, Andrea O'Reilly, *Remembering Cuba: Legacy of a Diaspora* (University of Texas Press, 2001).

Henderson, George Francis Robert, *Stonewall Jackson and the American Civil War*, Vol. 1 (Longmans, Green, and Co., 1909).

Hendrick, Burton J., *Statesmen Of The Lost Cause Jefferson Davis And His Cabinet* (New York: The Literary Guild of America, Inc., 1939).

Hood, John B., *Advance and Retreat, Personal Experiences in the United States and Confederate States Armies* (New Orleans: Hood Orphan Memorial Fund, 1880).

Hovey, Carl, *Stonewall Jackson* (Small, Maynard & Company, 1900).

Howell, Varina, *Jefferson Davis, Ex-President of the Confederate States of America: A Memoir*, Volume 2 (New York: Belford Company, Publishers,1890).

Hurst, Jack, *Nathan Bedford Forrest: A Biography* (Random House LLC, 1994).

Inman, Arthur C. ed., *Soldier of the South: General Pickett's War Letters to His Wife* (Boston & New York: Houghton Mifflin Company, 1928).

Jackson, H. W. E., *The Southern Women of the Second American Revolution, Their Trials & Yankee Barbarity Illustrated, Our Naval Victories and Exploits of Confederate War Steamers, Captures Yankee Gunboats* (Atlanta, Georgia: Intelligencer Steam-Power Press, 1863).

Jackson, Mary Anna, *Life and letters of General Thomas J. Jackson* (Harper & Brothers, 1892).

Jackson, Mary Anna, *Memoirs of Stonewall Jackson* (Louisville: The Prentice Press, 1895).

Jackson, Stonewall, *The life of Stonewall Jackson: From Official Papers, Contemporary Narratives, and Personal Acquaintance* (New York: Charles B. Richardson, 1864).

Johnson, Thomas Carry, *Life and Letters of Robert Lewis Dabney* (Richmond : The Presbyterian Committee of Publications, 1903).

Johnston, Mary, *The Long Role* (Toronto: Houghton Mifflin Company, 1911).

Johnston, Richard Malcolm and Browne, William Hand, *Life of Alexander H. Stephens* (Philadelphia: J. P. Lippincott & Company, 1878).

Johnston, William Preston, *The Life of Gen. Albert Sidney Johnston, Embracing His Services in the Armies of the United States, The Republic of Texas, and the Confederate States* (New York: D. Appleton Company, 1878).

Jones, J. William, *Christ In the Camp or Religion in Lee's Army* (Richmond: B. F. Johnson, 1887).

Jones, J. William, *Life and Letters of Robert Edward Lee, Soldier and Man* (New York: The Neale Publishing Company, 1906).

Jones, J. William, *Personal Reminiscences, Anecdotes, and Letters of General Robert E. Lee* (New York: D. Appleton & Company, 1874).

Jones, Katharine M., *Heroines Of Dixie Confederate: Women Tell Their Story Of The War* (New York: The Bobbs-Merrill Company, Inc., 1955).

Jones, Wilmer L., *Generals in Blue and Gray*, Volume 2 (Stackpole Books, 2005).

Jordan, Thomas and Pryor, J P., *The Campaigns of Lieut.-Gen. N.B. Forrest, and of Forrest's Cavalry* (New Orleans, La.: Blelock & Company, 1868).

Kelly, C. Brian, *Best Little Ironies, Oddities, and Mysteries of the Civil War* (Cumberland House Publishing, 2000).

Kennedy, James Ronald, *The South was Right!* (Pelican Publishing, 1994).

Lee, Fitzhugh, *General Lee* (New York: D. Appleton & Company, 1913).

Lee, Robert Edward, *Recollections and Letters of General Robert E. Lee* (Doubleday, Page & Company, 1904).

Lee, Robert Edward, *Robert E. Lee Softer Side* (Pelican Publishing, 2007).

Lewis, William Terrell, *Genealogy of the Lewis Family in America: From the Middle of the Seventeenth Century Down to the Present Time* (Louisville: The Courier-Journal Job Printing Company).

Long, A. L., *Memoirs of Robert E. Lee: His Military and Personal History* (J. M. Stoddart & Company, 1887).

Mathes, James Harvey, *Great Commanders: General Forrest* (New York: D. Appleton & Company, 1902).

McCabe, James Dabney, *Life and Campaigns of General Robert E. Lee* (National Publishing Company, 1866).

McCarthy, Carlton, *Detailed Minutiae of Soldier Life in the Army of*

Northern Virginia, 1861-1865 (Richmond: B. F. Johnson Publishing Company, 1882).

McClelland, Henry B., *The Life and Campaigns of Major-General J.E.B. Stuart, Commander of the Cavalry of the Army of Northern Virginia* (New York: Houghton, Mifflin & Company, 1885).

McClellan, Henry B., *I Rode With JEB Stuart: The Life and Campaigns of Major General JEB Stuart* (Da Capo Press, 1994).

McGuire, John Francis, *The Irish In America* (New York: D & J Saldier & Company, 1880).

McGuire, Judith White, *General Robert E. Lee, the Christian Soldier* (Claxton, Remsen & Haffelfinger, 1873).

McKim, Randolph H., *Chaplain, A Soldier's Recollections: Leaves From the Diary of a Young Confederate* (Longmans, Green & Company, 1910).

McWhiney, Grady and Jamieson, Perry D., *Attack and Die: Civil War Military Tactics and the Southern Heritage* (University of Alabama Press, 1984).

Martin, Iain C., *The Quotable American Civil War* (Lyons Press, 2008).

Maxwell, Jerry H., *The Perfect Lion: The Life and Death of Confederate Artillerist John Pelham* (University of Alabama Press, 2011).

Monteiro, Aristides, *War Reminiscences By the Surgeon of Mosby's Command* (Richmond, Virginia, 1890).

Moore, Frank, *The Portrait Gallery of the War, Civil, Military, and Naval: A Biographical Record* (D. Van Nostrand, 1865).

Morton, John Watson, *The Artillery of Nathan Bedford Forrest's Cavalry: The Wizard of the Saddle* (Publishing house of the M. E. Church, South, Smith & Lamar, Agents, 1909).

Mosby, John S., Mosby's *War Reminiscences and Stuart's Cavalry Campaigns* (Boston: George A. Jones & Company, Publishers, 1887).

Nall, John Thomas, *God Save the South: And a Treasure Chest of Forbidden Information* (AuthorHouse, 2013).

Nolan, Alan T., *Lee Considered: General Robert E. Lee and Civil War History* (UNC Press Books, 1996).

Noll, Arthur Howard, *General Kirby Smith* (Sewanee, Tennessee: The University Press at the University of the South, 1907).

Norton, Frank H., *The Life of Alexander H. Stephens* (New York: John B. Alden, Publisher, 1886).

O'Brien, Cormac, *Secret Lives of the Civil War: What Your Teachers Never Told You about the War Between the States* (Quirk Books, 2007).

Page, Thomas Nelson, *Robert E. Lee: Man and Soldier* (New York: Charles Scribner's Sons, 1911).

Page, Thomas Nelson, *Robert E. Lee: The Southerner* (New York: Charles Scribner's Sons, 1908).

Page, Thomas Nelson, *The Works of Thomas Nelson Page*, Volume 18 (C. Scribner's Sons, 1912).

Pavlovsky, Arnold M., *Riding in Circles: J.E.B. Stuart and the Confederate Cavalry 1861-1862* (Arnold M. Pavlovsky, 2010).

Peele, W. J., *Lives of Distinguished North Carolinians* (The North Carolina Publishing Society, 1898).

Philips, Ulrich Bonnell, *The Life of Robert Toombs* (New York: The MacMillan Company, 1913).

Pickett, LaSalle Corbell, *Pickett and His Men* (Atlanta: The Foote and Davies Company, Printers and Binders, 1900).

Pollard, Edward A., *Lee and His Lieutenants: Comparing the Early Life, Public Services, and Campaigns of General Robert E. Lee and His Companion In Arms, With a Record of the Campaigns and Heroic Deeds* (New York: E. B. Treat and Company, 1867).

Pollard, Edward A., *Life of Jefferson Davis, Secret History of the Southern Confederacy, Gathered Behind the Scenes in Richmond* (Atlanta: National Publishing Company, 1869).

Polley, J. B., *Hood's Texas Brigade: Its Marches, Its Battles, Its Achievements* (New York: The Neale Publishing Company, 1910).

Pryor, Elizabeth Brown, *Reading the Man – A Portrait of Robert E. Lee Through His Private Letters* (New York: Penguin Group, 2007).

Purdue, Howell and Purdue, Elizabeth, *Pat Cleburne, Confederate General: A Definitive Biography* (Hill Jr. College Press, 1973).

Rafuse, Ethan Sepp, *Stonewall Jackson: A Biography* (ABC-CLIO, 2011).

Reagan, John H., *Memoirs, With Special Reference to Secession and the Civil War* (New York: The Neale Publishing Company, 1906).

Reagan, John H., *State of the Union. Speech of the Hon. John H. Reagan, of Texas* (Washington, D. C.: W. H. Moore, Printer, 1861).

Rhett, Robert Barnwell, *A Fire-eater Remembers: The Confederate Memoir of Robert Barnwell Rhett* (University of South Carolina Press, 2000).

Richard, J. Fraise, *The Florence Nightingale of the Southern Army; Experiences of Mrs. Ella K. Newsom, Confederate Nurse in the Great War of 1861-65* (New York: Broadway Publishing Company, 1914).

Riley, Elihu Samuel, *Stonewall Jackson: A Thesaurus of Ancedotes of and Incidents in the Life of Lieut. General Jonathan Jackson, C.S.A.* (Elihu Samuel Riley, 1920).

Riley, Franklin L., *General Robert E. Lee after Appomattox* (New York:

MacMillian Company, 1922).

Rister, Carl Coke, *Robert E. Lee in Texas* (University of Oklahoma Press, 1946).

Roberson, Elizabeth Whitley, *Weep Not for Me, Dear Mother* (Pelican Publishing, 1996).

Robertson, James I., *The Stonewall Brigade* (LSU Press, 1978).

Rose, Victor M., *The Life and Services of General Benjamin Bullouch* (Philadelphia: Pictorial Bureau, 1888).

Russell, Charles Wells, *The Memoirs of Colonel John S. Mosby* (Bloomington: Indiana University Press, 1959).

Santayana, George, *The Life of Reason and the Phases of Human Progress* (New York: Charles Scribner's Sons, 2012).

Scharf, J. Thomas, *History of the Confederate States Navy from Its Organization to the Surrender of Its Last Vessel* (New York: Rogers & Sherwood, 1887).

Sedore, Timothy S., *An Illustrated Guide to Virginia's Confederate Monuments* (SIU Press, April 29, 2011).

Selby, John, *Stonewall Jackson as Military Commander* (Barnes & Noble Publishing, 1968).

Sigaud, Louis A., *Belle Boyd Confederate Spy* (Richmond: The Dietz Press, Incorporated, 1945).

Smith, John David, Appleton, Thomas H., Roland, Charles Pierce, *A Mythic Land Apart: Reassessing Southerners and Their History* (Greenwood Publishing Group, 1997).

Snow, William Parker, *Lee and His Generals* (New York: The Fairfax Press, 1982).

Snow, William Parker, *Southern General: Their Lives and Campaigns* (New York: Charles B. Richardson, 1866).

Spencer, Cornelia Phillips, *The Last Ninety Days of the War in North Carolina* (New York: Watchman Publishing Company, 1866).

Stevenson, Burton Egbert, *The Home Book of Verse, American and English 1580-1918* (New York: Henry Holt & Company, 1918).

Stovall, Pleasant A., *Robert Toombs: Statesmen, Speaker, Soldier, Sage* (New York: Cassell Publishing Company, 1892).

Strode, Hudson, *Jefferson Davis: Confederate President* (New York: Harcourt, Brace and Company, 1950).

Tanner, Robert G., *Stonewall in the Valley: Thomas J. 'Stonewall' Jackson's Shenandoah Valley Campaign, Spring 1862* (Stackpole Books, 2002).

Tate, Allen, *Stonewall Jackson: The Good Soldier* (Rowman & Littlefield, 1991).

Thomas, Emory M., *Bold Dragon: The Life of JEB Stuart* (University of Oklahoma Press, 1999).

Thomas, Emory M., *Robert E. Lee: A Biography* (W. W. Norton & Company, 1997).

Thomason, John William, *JEB Stuart* (University of Nebraska Press, 1994).

Trout, Robert J., *They Followed the Plume: The Story of J.E.B. Stuart and His Staff* (Stackpole Books, 2003).

Trudeau, Noah Andre, *Robert E. Lee* (MacMillan, 2009).

Tucker, Spencer, *Brigadier General John D. Imboden: Confederate Commander in the Shenandoah* (University Press of Kentucky, 2010).

Underwood, Rodman L., *Stephen Russell Mallory: A Biography of the Confederate Navy Secretary and United States Senator* (McFarland, 2005).

Vaughan, C. R., Editor, *Discussions By Robert Lewis Dabney*, Volume 4 (Mexico, Mo.: Crescent Book House, 1897).

Von Abele, Rudolph, *Alexander H Stephens: A Biography* (New York: Alfred A. Knopf, 1946).

Walsh, George, *Damage Them All You Can: Robert E. Lee's Army of Northern Virginia* (Macmillan, 2003).

Wert, Jeffry D., *Gettysburg, Day Three* (Simon and Schuster, 2002).

Wert, Jeffry D., *Cavalryman of the Lost Cause: A Biography of J. E. B. Stuart* (Simon and Schuster, 2009).

Ward, Geoffrey C., *The Civil War* (Random House LLC, 1994).

White, Henry Alexander, *Robert E. Lee and the Southern Confederacy, 1807-1870* (New York: G.P. Putman's Sons, 1897).

White, Henry Alexander, *Stonewall Jackson* (G. W. Jacobs, 1909).

Wilkins, J. Steven, *Call of Duty: The Sterling Nobility of Robert E. Lee* (Cumberland House Publishing, 1997), 183.

Williams, Richard G. Jr., *Maxims of Robert E. Lee for Young Gentlemen* (Pelican Publishing, 2005).

Williamson, James J., *Mosby's Rangers: A Record of the Operations of the Forty-Third Battalion of Virginia Cavalry From Its Organization to the Surrender* (New York: Sturgis & Walton Company, 1909).

Williamson, Mary L., *The life of J. E. B. Stuart* (Richmond: B.F. Johnson & Company, 1914).

Williamson, Mary L., *Life of Robert E. Lee* (Richmond: Johnson Publishing Company, 1918).

Wills, Brian Steel, *A Battle From the Start: The life of Nathan Bedford Forrest* (HarperPerennial, 1993).

Winkler, C. M., *The Life and Character of General John B. Hood* (Austin, Texas: Droughon & Lambert, Printer, 1885).

Woods, Jr., Thomas E., *33 Questions About American History You're Not Supposed to Ask* (Random House LLC, 2007).

Woodworth, Steven E., *The Loyal, True, and Brave: America's Civil War Soldiers* (Rowman & Littlefield, 2002).

Worthington, C. J. Editor, *The Woman In Battle: A Narrative of the Exploits, Adventure, and Travels of Madame Loretta Janeta Velasquez, Otherwise Known As Harry T. Buford, Confederate States Army* (Hartford: T. Belknap, 1876).

Wyeth, John Allan, *Life of General Nathan Bedford Forrest* (New York: Harper & Brothers, 1899).

Wyeth, John Allan, *Life of Lieutenant-General Nathan Bedford Forrest* (New York: Harper & Brothers Publishers, 1908).

Wyeth, John Allan, *That Devil Forrest: Life of General Nathan Bedford Forrest* (LSU Press, 1989).

Index

Alexander, Edward Porter, 86
Anderson, M. D., 128
Andrews, Eliza Frances, 98
Armistead, Lewis A., 88

Beauregard, Pierre Gustave Toutant, 84
Bee, Barnard, 90
Benjamin, Judah Philip, 17
Bennett, W. T., 134
Boyd, Isabelle "Belle," 97, 98, 99
Bradford, Susan, 106
Brown, Albert Gallatin, 27
Byson, Mary, 113

Campbell, A. B., 124
Campbell, J. H., 122
Carlisle, J. M., 122
Chesnut, Mary Boykin, 85, 102
Cleburne, Patrick Ronayne, 65, 66, 70
Cline, J. M., 135
Clopton, J. C., 119
Cook, J. O. A., 126
Cranberry, J. C., 127
Cross, Joseph, 130
Cumming, Kate, 109

Dabney, Robert Lewis, 46, 51, 88
Davis, George, 26
Davis, Jefferson, 7, 8, 9, 10, 22, 26, 106
Davis, Varina Howell, 106
Dawson, Sarah Morgan, 104
De La Coste, Marie Ravenel, 112
de Treville, Mary Darby, 106
Dunlap, W. C., 132

Elder, Susan Blanchard, 105

Fitzgerald, Frederick, 137
Forrest, Nathan Bedford, 72, 73, 74, 75, 76, 77, 78, 79, 80

Gay, Mary Ann Harris, 101
Greenhow, Rose O'Neal, 103

Hampton, Wade, 46, 71
Hanson, Roger Weightman, 89
Hatcher, Hilary E., 128
Hauser, William, 133
Henry, Gustavus A., 30
Hiden, James Conway, 120
Hill, Daniel Harvey, 90
Hobby, Alfred Marmaduke, 91
Hood, John Bell, 67
Howerton, S. W., 124
Hunter, Robert Mercer Taliaferro, 16
Hyman, J. J., 123

Imboden, John Daniel, 87

Jackson, Mary Anna, 48, 51, 53, 54, 57, 107
Jackson, Thomas Jonathan, 47, 50, 51, 53, 54, 57
Johnston, Albert Sidney, 64, 102, 103
Johnston, P. A., 133
Jones, J. William, 37, 38, 39, 40, 41, 42, 43, 44, 46, 47, 49, 51, 117, 118, 123, 124, 129, 131, 132
Jones, W. E., 135

Kollock, Augusta J., 108
Kundera, Milan, 1

Lacy, Beverly Tucker, 117
Landers, Eli Pinson, 90
Leachman, J. D., 127
Lee, Richard Henry, 91

Lee, Robert Edward, 37. 38, 40, 41, 42, 43
Loughborough, Mary Ann, 111

Manly, Basil, 117
Martin, J. E., 122
Maury, Betty Herndon, 109
McCarthy, Carlton, 87
McCulloch, Benjamin, 90
McDonald, Cornelia Peake, 97
McGuire, Judith White, 42, 99
McKim, Randolph H., 137, 138
McVeigh, T. J., 121
McVoy, Alexander Diego, 136
Mallory, Stephen Russell, 23
Memminger, Christopher Gustavus, 17
Meynardie, E. J., 132
Miller, C. W., 136
Mills, J. W., 127
Morgan, John Hunt, 85
Mosby, John Singleton, 59, 85, 86

Newsom, Ella King, 107

Oldham, Williamson Simpson, 28
Owen, W. B., 118

Pelham, John, 88
Pickett, George Edward, 84
Pike, Albert, 81
Porter, Florence May, 107
Porter, R. G., 135

Quintard, Charles Todd, 134

Reagan, John Henninger, 19
Renfroe, J. J. D., 125
Rhett, Robert Barnwell, 27
Roach, J. M. B., 121

Ryland, Robert, 128

Sansom, Emma, 111
Scales, Cordelia Lewis, 111
Sims, Leora, 109
Smith, Edmund Kirby, 82
Smith, Lucy, 110
Smith, Samuel S., 132
Smith, W. H., 134
Spencer, Cornelia Phillips, 97
Stephens, A. B., 136
Stephens, Alexander Hamilton, 11
Stiles, Joseph C., 129
Stinson, Virginia McCollum, 113
Stokes, J. M., 123
Strick, S., 133
Strough, A. L., 121
Stuart, James Ewell Brown, 41, 57, 58, 59, 60, 61, 62, 63

Tansil, Robert, 89
Tichnor, Isaac Taylor, 131
Tomkies, John H., 124
Toombs, Robert Augustus, 14, 15, 16

Unknown Southern Woman, 106

Velasquez, Loretta Janeta, 100, 101

Wadley, Sarah Lois, 110
Walker, Leroy Pope, 22
Watkins, Sam R., 89
Watts, Thomas Hill, 2, 24
Wheeler, Joseph, 86
Wiatt, William E., 125
Wilson, Reuben Everett, 90
Woodfin, A. B., 126

Yancey, Willam Lowndes, 32
Yarbrough, E. W., 131